THE MILLION-DOLLAR
FINANCIAL ADVISOR

The Million-Dollar Financial Advisor

Powerful Lessons and Proven Strategies from Top Producers

DAVID J. MULLEN, JR.

HARPERCOLLINS
LEADERSHIP

AN IMPRINT OF HARPERCOLLINS

The Million-Dollar Financial Advisor

Published by HarperCollins Leadership, an imprint of HarperCollins Focus LLC.

Any internet addresses, phone numbers, or company or product information printed in this book are offered as a resource and are not intended in any way to be or to imply an endorsement by HarperCollins Leadership, nor does HarperCollins Leadership vouch for the existence, content, or services of these sites, phone numbers, companies, or products beyond the life of this book.

Bulk discounts available. For details visit:
www.harpercollinsleadership.com/bulkquotes
Email: customercare@harpercollins.com

ISBN 978-1-4002-3880-4 (TP)

To my parents: the late Dave, Sr., and Rosemary Mullen. Not only were they wonderful parents, but both were teachers who inspired me to share knowledge with others.

CONTENTS

PART 2: PUTTING THE LESSONS INTO PRACTICE

ACKNOWLEDGMENTS

To my loving family, for providing their unconditional love and support. Thank you Cynthia, Katie, John, David, and Nathan.

I would also like to thank the top advisors I had the privilege of working with and talking to about their extraordinary business practices. They unselfishly gave their time so that my readers could benefit from their hard-earned lessons. These top advisors are among the best role models the financial services industry has.

I would like to thank my agent, Wendy Keller and AMACOM for believing in this book. My editor Bob Shuman did great work with the manuscript. And thanks to Pam Liflander for being my editing partner in this book, providing her services to make the most of my work.

THE MILLION-DOLLAR
FINANCIAL ADVISOR

Introduction

I HAVE ALWAYS had an insatiable curiosity about the methods successful people use to reach the pinnacle of their industry. I am particularly interested in the financial services field, because this is where I have made my career. When I started in the business back in 1980, my goal was to create my own million-dollar practice, but I had absolutely no idea how to do it. I read all the literature at the time about how to be successful, but there didn't seem to be any blueprint for me to follow. Even though I was motivated to succeed, I knew that the odds were against me: Only one percent of those who start in this business ever reach the million-dollar business level.

So began the long, challenging journey toward my goal. I spent the first six years of my career as a financial advisor, starting in 1980 with a large, national financial services firm in my hometown of Athens, Georgia. I was 25 years old and had absolutely no idea how to build a financial services practice. I didn't know anyone who had more than $20,000 to invest and had never sold an intangible product before. I was as green as they get, but I did have a high level of motivation to succeed. I soon recognized this business was much more difficult than I had expected and that I was in for the biggest challenge of my life. Through hard work, perseverance, and a little luck, I began building my business, growing it bigger every year.

While developing my practice, I realized that I wanted to help others thrive as well. I was given my first opportunity to help other financial advisors back in 1984, when I was promoted to the level of producing manager in a large, national financial services firm in Atlanta. I took my best accounts with me and threw myself at the challenge. I was in charge of motivating a group of unsuspecting financial advisors. What I lacked in managerial experience I made up for in energy and enthusiasm. I began to teach the lessons that I had learned to those reporting to me, to great results. In just two years that office cumulatively grew by almost 30 percent.

Then, in 1986, I passed the firm's assessment for managers, and my dream of having a full-time career helping other financial advisors came true. Over the next 20 years I had managerial responsibilities in Denver, Newport Beach, Minneapolis, New York City, and Atlanta. In every location I was sent I saw the same thing: I realized that there was much to be learned, but saw how little was shared. So I started to collect and refine a set of best business practices for this industry. These lessons are featured in my first book, *The Million-Dollar Financial Services Practice*, which provides the fundamentals to guide any financial advisor to a million-dollar business, no matter where you are in your financial services career.

Learning from the Masters

If my first book is the equivalent of a college degree in financial services, then this new one is the graduate course. The first book was designed to be a tactical blueprint for success, but the next step was to focus on the proven lessons that could be learned from many of the top advisors in the industry. The combination of these two books should provide instruction as well as the motivation needed to help you reach your goals. These lessons can be incorporated at any stage of your financial career; in fact, the earlier they are understood and followed, the better.

During my 20-year management career, I was privileged to meet some of the very best and brightest in the financial services industry. In fact, I recruited, hired, and eventually worked with more than 100 individuals who were "million plus" financial advisors. Through this experience I was able observe the best practices of these top financial advisors and compare them to the best practices I had developed. I was surprised to see how much more I still had to learn. Then I realized the challenge most advisors face: They simply don't have access to individuals they can learn from. There is little flow of information downward because top advisors are extremely focused on their own practices.

However, I was able to interview 15 professionals who have personally exemplified what it takes to be at the very top. Through my personal and professional relationships with them, I was able to observe and interview them, asking them the questions that I know you would want to ask on exactly how they were able to become so successful. I had also worked directly with most of these advisors for years and was able to watch them, in many instances, practicing these lessons "live." The combination of the interviews, my personal interactions with these professionals, and my knowledge and experience is what separates this book from all others.

The Million-Dollar Financial Advisor provides a rare glimpse into the best practices that make these top producers so successful. All of the information in this book was acquired through in-depth interviews and, in many cases, years of observations while working with these top advisors. I am confident that this wealth of information makes this book unique.

Each of these top advisors' achievements went beyond a million-dollar practice. In all cases these exceptional men and women became successful "the old-fashion way." No one handed them a book of business or gave them special treatment: They all started at the bottom and built their multimillion-dollar businesses from scratch. In all cases they started with nothing. With no related experience, they made the same mistakes all rookies make; they had to reinvent the wheel. In each case, however, their motivation, determination, goal focus, and hard work carried them through each obstacle that they faced to get to the next level. My purpose was to discover the principles of success that they all had in common and translate that into "lessons" for readers to take their business to the next level.

You now have access to these top advisors. All of them have shared their insights graciously and openly. You will learn from their mistakes as well as their successes. And while it does not guarantee a multimillion-dollar practice, it can certainly raise your level of productivity. For example, I would often send the advisors in the offices that I managed to visit with higher producers in the same company, and I was always pleased by the significant lift in returns that would result.

The Million-Dollar Financial Advisor was written for financial advisors who want to take their business practice to the next level. The information I obtained from my extensive interviews has been organized into 13 distinct lessons that these top advisors followed. The guidelines should be used as a checklist to compare yourself with the best in the business. In some cases the lessons should be a confirmation of what you are currently doing right; in other cases, they will identify a gap in your business practice that needs to be developed. What's more, this book provides the specific steps that you can take in order to implement the lessons.

The careers of our top advisors have spanned from 7 to 40 years. They have thrived during bull markets and survived during the bear markets. Their lessons have withstood the test of time and are applicable in any market environment. As we've seen from recent economic events, markets have and always will change, but the lessons from these top advisors stay the same. The lessons from these top advisors will guide you to the top, too, no matter the current market conditions.

I have also included two complete case studies that are of particular interest. First, you will meet Taylor Glover, whom I consider to be the most successful financial advisor I have ever met. From my interview with him, you will learn how the "best of the best" built his business and how he advanced from a newly minted advisor to the No. 1 producer in his firm. This case study also illustrates how all of the lessons work together and what the results can be.

A second study illustrates a unique financial advisor who has turned his career around. Henry Camp teaches us the value of hard work and incredible perseverance and should serve as an inspiration to anyone who desires to become a multimillion-dollar financial advisor, no matter what career stage he or she is in.

The final chapter offers a specific challenge: to use these lessons and drive your practice to financial success. By implementing these lessons, you will understand how to significantly increase your assets and your business. The Asset Challenge serves as an example of what the implementation of the lessons from the top can produce. Some advisors will exceed the goal and others may not reach it, but those advisors that follow the tactical strategies outlined in this chapter on a consistent basis will take their business practice to the next and higher level.

Meet the Top Advisors

This book was not created by simply compiling data. I have known each and every one of our top advisors for years and have watched their best practices from a front-row seat. Working with these men and women was simply the best, most effective training available for me, and now I can pass this information on to you.

The criteria to be included as a top advisor was simple: Their business needed to generate in excess of $3 million annually, with no compliance issues, and built from scratch. There were two exceptions to the business minimum, and in both cases the circumstances warranted a lower number because of the smaller markets that they produced in. However, in both of these cases, their individual production was between $2 million and $3 million. Although I did not include every $3 million-plus advisor I had ever known or worked with, the ones I did choose were exceptional in every way. I let the quality of the advisor and criteria dictate the number of participants, which turned out to be 15 individuals who built exceptional businesses.

These top advisors are ordinary individuals who, through determination, have become among the best in the financial services business. They come from a diversity of backgrounds, representing different genders, races, ages, and locations. I found that external factors like their office location and size played a minimal role in their success. However, their internal drive and focus played a paramount role. Besides having an interesting story, all of the top advisors have a unique approach to both clients and the services they provide.

One fact that came out of the selection process was that for financial services, the old real estate adage of "location, location, location" simply doesn't matter. The 15 top advisors have their offices located in all parts of the country, from the Southeast to California, and from New York to the Rocky Mountain West and the Midwest. Five of the most successful advisors are located in the Southeast and Midwest, dispelling the notion that the largest population centers produce the most successful advisors. They practice in a broad range of locations: from large metropolitan areas to smaller cities.

Just as location wasn't a limiting factor, neither was gender and race. These top advisors would be the first to tell you that they were determined not to let race or gender limit their ability to succeed. In all cases they turned potential disadvantages into advantages. Time after time, their stories show that they never made excuses; they knew they were responsible for reaching their goals no matter the challenges.

However, to protect their privacy, the names of the top advisors have been changed. In order to get the candor and depth of information these advisors provided, I felt I needed to protect their real identities. This arrangement allowed them to more freely share how they acquired new relationships, and to reveal their marketing and business tactics and be open about their numbers. In many cases they provided the exact verbiage they use to acquire clients. The two exceptions I made were in the case of Taylor Glover and Henry Camp, who have both retired and no longer provide professional financial advice.

The Interview Process

The interviewing process was conducted with you, the reader, in mind. I asked the questions I believed you would want to ask if you had three hours to spend with each top advisor.

The interviews were structured around 70 specific questions. Some of the interviewees spent more time on different questions, but in the end every advisor answered every question to my satisfaction. As the interviews progressed, I began to identify the common success principles, which I refer to throughout as "lessons," that the top advisors all had in common.

Interestingly, I found that each of our top advisors was pleased to be included in the book. Their motivation came from a genuine interest in making a positive difference in the careers of other advisors who could benefit from their success. Each of these people started their careers without a clue as to how to build a successful practice. They agreed that if they had received a book like this when they were starting out, it would have saved them a great deal of time in building a successful practice. By participating, they all felt that this was their way to contribute back to an industry that had provided them the opportunity to reach a level of success that probably would not have been reached any other way.

Top Advisor Questionnaire

Here's what we asked them:

- What was your background coming into this business? What were your college and major?

- Describe your early years in the business.

- What do you do best? What are your challenges?

- What do you believe has accounted for your success in building a multimillion-dollar practice?

- What do you consider the qualities that have led to your success?

- How do you see yourself as different from other advisors?

- Did you have a vision from the beginning as how you were going to grow your business?

- How did it evolve? What is your vision now for your business?

- How did you start out prospecting? What worked? How has your marketing evolved?

- How did you get your biggest clients?

- Do you prospect socially? How do you transition from personal to business relationships?

- How did you meet your largest clients? How did you turn them from prospects to clients?

- Why do you think people do business with you?

- What advice would you offer an aspiring million-dollar advisor?

- Is there anything you would do differently if you could do it over again?

- In the past, have you been involved in nonprofit organizations? Were you able to translate that involvement into business? How?

- Do you have a specialization? What do you consider your expertise?

- What is your investment philosophy? How do you implement it for your clients? Do you consider yourself a wealth manager (i.e., using a holistic approach) as opposed to an investment generalist?

- How many relationships do you work with directly? How many million-dollar relationships do you have? Do you have a minimum size? What is the average asset size/revenue amount of your clients?

- How is your team structured? How has it evolved? How does your team support your efforts?

- How do you find time for your family? How do you maintain quality of life?

- How many hours a week do you work? Has that changed over the years?

- How do you structure your time? What is your typical day like?

- How do you fit it all in?

- What percentage of your time do you spend with clients and prospects?

- Are you still actively marketing? What percentage of your time is spent on marketing activities?

❏ Describe your outside interests. How do you tie those interests into business?

❏ Describe your assets. How many assets do you manage? How much business did you do last year? Annualized this year? What is your five-year growth rate? How many new assets do you bring in a year? What is the biggest source of new assets? How long have you been in the business?

❏ Do you have a network of influencers, and how did you develop that network? How many referrals do you get annually?

❏ How would you describe your attitude (mindset) as it relates to the business?

❏ Describe your relationship with your clients. Describe the kind of leadership you provide your clients.

❏ What is your client service philosophy? How do you service your clients? Has your client service attitude evolved?

❏ How much of your own money do you spend on your practice? How is it spent?

❏ What keeps you up at night as it relates to your business? Do you enjoy the business? What gives you the greatest satisfaction?

What We Learned from the Data

The average age of a top advisor is 52, with the youngest being 38 and the oldest 64. There was no correlation between the amount of business done and their age or their experience level—in other words, the oldest and most experienced didn't necessarily do the most business. Their average length of service in the industry was 26 years. Most of these advisors started their careers in financial services as either their first or second job. The average age for starting in this business was 25 years old. The majority went to public, state-sponsored undergraduate colleges or universities; none attended an Ivy League university. Only two of the 15 men and women had continued their education with graduate school, and both were MBAs.

Most of the top advisors came from modest beginnings. Their parents were school teachers, plant supervisors, small business owners, farmers, salesmen, and service military. They built their businesses from scratch; they were given nothing; and there were no special circumstances beyond themselves that accounted for their success.

Their business, at year-end for 2008, ranged from $2 million to $15 million, with the average being $5 million. While many of the top advisors were part of a team and split business, I only credited the advisors with their individual level of business: The total team business was not included. The assets under management ranged from $500 million to $4 billion, with the average being $1 billion. Their velocity rate was an average of .50 basis points (business divided by assets—100bp equals 1 percent). The velocity rate is also referred to as ROA, or return on assets. In some cases there were large concentrated positions of stock among some of their clients, which lowered the velocity rate. The top advisors with fewer total relationships had a lower velocity rate because the size of each relationship was bigger and, as a percentage of assets, generated less business.

The number of relationships that each advisor worked with directly ranged from 20 to 200, with the average number being 80 clients. There was a correlation between the size of the markets and the number of relationships the advisor worked with: The smaller the market, the more relationships the top advisor maintained. In each case the top advisor had set a minimum size relationship, which ranged from $500,000 to $100 million, with the average minimum being $1 million. In smaller markets, the minimum size was lower than in the larger markets. In most cases the minimum relationship was at least $1 million, so the number of total relationships was very close to the number of million-dollar-plus relationships. Although their minimums might be stated, each of the top advisors would accept clients with lower assets under certain circumstances. It is important to note that Taylor Glover, the top advisor profiled in Chapter 14, was taken out of the statistics. His numbers are astronomical—he did twice the business of the second highest top advisor—and therefore his numbers would have distorted the averages.

Our top advisors are continuously focused on marketing and the acquisition of new assets and client relationships that meet their minimums, regardless of the economic outlook. In 2008, the range of new assets brought in spanned from $25 million to $400 million, with the average being $50 million. The $400 million was taken out of the average calculation because it would have distorted the averages. Most of these advisors stated that $50 million in new assets a year was their goal, and that goal was usually met.

These success lessons will stand the test of time, no matter the market conditions.

The Top Advisors

Here are the profiles of our top advisors, including their financial statistics.

Dana—$3 million in business, $500 million in assets. Length of service (LOS): 26 years. Specialization: working with high-net-worth individuals valued at $1 million or more. Total relationships: 100. Known for her commitment to the not-for-profit world; has a high level of expertise in philanthropy. Location: West.

Mike—$5 million in business, $1 billion in assets. LOS: 14 years. Specialization: working with high-net-worth families of $10 million or more. Total relationships: 50. Location: Southeast.

John—$7 million in business, $2 billion in assets. LOS: 30 years. Specialization: working with high-net-worth families of $10 million or more. Total relationships: 80. Location: Southeast.

Sam—$4 million in business, $2 billion in assets. LOS: 25 years. Specialization: working with high-net-worth families and corporate services of $10 million or more. Total relationships: 60. Location: Southeast.

David—$2.5 million in business, $1 billion in assets. LOS: 30 years. Specialization: institutional consulting services and large retirement plans. Total relationships: 48. Location: Southeast.

Jack—$3 million in business, $750 million in assets. LOS: 40 years. Specialization: physicians, retirement plans, affluent individuals. Total relationships: 200. Location: Southeast.

Greg—$3 million in business, $1 billion in assets. LOS: 40 years. Specialization: high-net-worth individuals of $1 million plus. Total relationships: 200. Location: Northeast.

Joseph—$7 million in business, $1 billion in assets. LOS: 26 years. Specialization: physicians, retirement plans, high-net-worth individuals of $1 million plus. Total relationships: 200. Location: Midwest.

Rob—$7 million in business, $1.4 billion in assets. LOS: 31 years. Specialization: entrepreneurs and high-net-worth individuals over $10 million. Total relationships: 78. Location: Midwest.

Ross—$3 million in business, $700 million in assets. LOS: 26 years. Specialization: private business owners and senior executives; average account size $2.5 million. Total relationships: 120. Location: West.

Anne—$4 million in business, $1.3 billion in assets. LOS: 7 years. Specialization: senior executives and private business owners. Total relationships: 62. Location: West.

William—$2 million in business, $500 million in assets. LOS: 29 years. Specialization: retirement plans, affluent individuals. Total relationships: 200. Location: Midwest.

Charles—$3 million in business, $500 million in assets. LOS: 15 years. Specialization: professional referral sources. Total relationships: 100. Location: West.

Henry—$3.5 million in business, $1 billion in assets. LOS: 32 years. Specialization: corporate services and senior executives. Location: Southeast.

Taylor—consistently produced over $10 million during the five years prior to his retirement, with a career high of $15 million, and $4 billion in assets. LOS: 30 years. Specialization: working with ultra high-net-worth individuals and families; worked directly with 10 to 20 relationships of $100 million or more. Location: Southeast (Atlanta).

Top Advisor Lessons Summarized

Building a successful practice is an evolution, not a revolution, and identifying what strategies and techniques are missing from your business is the first step. The following chapters will each explore one of the success principles, with anecdotes from the top advisors that illustrate how they have applied these lessons and how you can implement them, too. Briefly, here are the lessons you'll discover.

THE MINDSET

Our top advisors all have a common mindset toward the business, and many have common personality traits. They operate with a high level of *confidence*. They provide an aura of being at the top of their game. They are very *competitive*; they know their exact business numbers and rankings among their peers. They have been *goal-oriented* throughout their career, and remain that way even though they are at the top of their game: They continue to have aspirations to do more and become better. When asked what their goals were they could articulate them immediately and succinctly. These objectives were part of a greater *vision* that they had for their business. From the beginning of their careers, they've had a *strong work ethic*. Most of these top advisors are still putting in 50 hours a week. They keep their *energy* levels high, as well as their *passion* for business. These top advisors are *leaders* and provide leadership to their team and clients. Throughout their careers they have shown personal *courage* by being willing to risk failure to achieve success. They are excellent one-on-one *communicators* with a sincere interest in helping people and putting the needs of their clients ahead of themselves. Because their concern for their clients is their first priority—and their ethics are beyond reproach—their clients and prospects instinctively trust them; *trustworthiness* contributes greatly to their success.

LEVERAGE OF SIZE

Our top advisors understand that leverage in financial services is based on the size of the relationships: the amount of assets each client has invested with each advisor. This is far more important than the total number of relationships under management. These men and women didn't start out understanding this concept, but they all evolved to adopt it. In the beginning, most of these advisors focused on the number of new accounts they opened, without regard to size, but as their careers progressed they kept raising the minimums and reducing the total number of client relationships. They all learned that it doesn't take any more time to invest $1 million in assets than $100,000, but the payoff is ten times greater. By working with fewer highly affluent clients, these advisors provide the time required to service them while still generating a large volume of business.

PROFESSIONAL DEVELOPMENT

As the top advisors told their stories, it became clear that they recognized early on the need to set themselves apart from the competition. They devoted time and resources to be the best. Whether it was professional designations, ongoing education, or searching for better and more efficient business practices, these advisors continued to be students of the game. They never quit learning. They were students of the markets, always working to provide the best investment advice possible to their clients. They had an insatiable appetite for the business, looking at it as more than just a job.

SPECIALIZATION

Typically, our top advisors started out as generalists, casting a wide net to find whatever clients they could. But over time they all developed a specialization and expertise in a particular niche. Their focus might be with a particular occupation, such as working with senior executives, or focusing on retirement planning. They have found that the barrier to entry into a specific market is high for the average financial advisor, so in a sense they have "cornered the market" in their area of expertise.

RELATIONSHIP FOCUS

Our top advisors are master relationship builders. They spend the vast majority of their time communicating, socializing, and being with affluent clients and prospects. These advisors have excellent one-on-one people skills. They are attuned to the needs of affluent investors, are excellent listeners, and as a result, are well liked and trusted. They are patient and willing to commit the necessary time and energy to develop meaningful relationships with their clients and prospects. These top advisors understand it is fundamentally a people, not a numbers, business.

MARKETING

The top advisors have been actively marketing themselves for their entire careers. As a result, their businesses have never stopped growing. Their primary methods of marketing include client referrals, professional referral networks, client events, nonprofit leadership, right place and right people (being in a position to meet affluent people and over time transitioning to business relationships), and niche marketing. Many times their marketing efforts occurred outside of business hours. These advisors believe that there is a fine line between work and play, and they like it that way.

PROFESSIONAL REFERRAL NETWORK

The number-one way that millionaires choose their financial advisor is through their CPA and/or attorney, whom we call *professional referral sources*. The top advisors all recognize the marketing leverage of developing a network of referring professionals. They developed these relationships primarily through the CPAs and attorneys of their best clients, and over time cultivated this network to provide them consistent referrals.

NONPROFIT ORGANIZATIONS

Taking a leadership role in a local or national not-for-profit organization—including performing arts, civic, alumni, and health care organizations—is a consistent trait among the top advisors. The shared strategy was that they could showcase their talents and investment expertise for the nonprofits and meet many of the most prominent and influential members of the community at the same time. Being a leader in these organizations gave them exposure to these highly affluent prospects and the opportunity to build relationships around a mutual interest.

LONG-TERM ORIENTATION

The top advisors realized early on that if they were going to focus on bigger relationships they would have to be patient. The most affluent investors have many different options and are the target of every financial services firm. Relationships with highly affluent prospects take time to develop, and top advisors take whatever time is required to develop these relationships. This long-term orientation doesn't just apply to prospects; it also means taking a long-term view of investing for and servicing their clients.

THE TEAM

All of our top advisors are the senior partners on their team and maintain the largest percentage of the team's business. In some cases they are the only team member with a book of business. These are all vertical teams, with the team built to support the top advisor. In all cases they evolved over time; the team that is in place now is different from the teams they had or were part of early in their careers. They are very respectful of their team members and compensate them generously for good performance. As a result, there is a high level of loyalty from the team, as well as respect for the top advisors. In all cases there was at least one senior assistant working directly with them. In most cases there is a succession plan in place, because it is important to these advisors that their clients and team members be taken care of in the event of their departure from the business. The priority of the team is to enable the top advisor to do what this person does best, which is spending time with the most important clients and prospecting new relationships. Recognizing the importance of a great team, the advisors are willing to pay whatever it takes to create them. Many of their teams are among the highest paid in the industry.

WEALTH MANAGEMENT

The top advisors consider themselves to be wealth managers; they take a comprehensive, holistic approach to investment management. They position themselves as being the advisor that takes care of each and every one of their client's financial needs, from portfolio management to liability management, asset protection, banking, and retirement and estate planning. In all cases the advisors evolved to this position from being a "stock broker" or someone who just handled the investment portion of the relationship. As these advisors grew their practices, they recognized the profitability of servicing other areas and expanding their advisor role into those areas. In many cases these advisors serve as a family office for their best clients. They are committed to frequent client communication that includes monthly contact, quarterly reviews, and annual reviews.

SERVICE COMMITMENT

Only good things happen when affluent clients are satisfied. They bring in more assets, provide referrals, follow their advisor's recommendations, and don't leave. These advisors recognize that to provide outstanding service for highly affluent clients, they have to limit the number of clients they work with. They also provide a service experience that is unique in their market area. In some cases it meant adding a fully paid assistant, providing the team with needed technology, and attracting and retaining the talent needed to provide extraordinary service. These advisors recognize that an outstanding service experience is often what differentiates them from their competition, and it is sometimes just as important as investment performance.

TIME MANAGEMENT

Our top advisors spend the majority of their time every day with their clients and prospective clients, and they delegate the majority of their nonrelationship tasks to their team. They don't spend much time with other financial advisors in the office, because in their view that takes time away from their clients and prospects. Willing to work long hours, the majority of their hours are spent productively—with affluent people.

Moving Forward

As you read through the rest of the book, you'll come to know each of these top advisors. You'll learn from their mistakes, and celebrate their successes. Best of all, you'll be able to incorporate the lessons they have learned into your own business. It is important to see how these lessons can work together to make your business extremely profitable and help you stand out in this very competitive industry.

PART ONE: THE LESSONS

PART ONE: THE LESSON

1

The Top Advisor Mindset

THE WORD *MINDSET* refers to our attitude or personality. It describes our mental wiring. A mindset represents a way of thinking, which can either be an innate response or character traits that can be developed. Your mindset can contain a host of variables, including whether you are laid back or aggressive, focused or scattered, "Type A" or "Type B," practical or passionate.

Developing a top advisor mindset is a distinct strategy that can be implemented to elevate your practice. In fact, it is probably the most important principle to tackle. Without the right attitude, none of the other success principles can exist. Your mindset drives everything else in your business; it forms the foundation from which highly successful careers are built. There is nothing easy about attaining the right frame of mind, but the top advisors will tell you that the rewards far exceed the work required.

The top advisors shared every one of the following traits:

▫ Confidence

▫ Professionalism

▫ Competitiveness

▫ Goal Orientation

▫ Vision

▫ Strong Work Ethic

▫ Energy

▫ Passion

▫ Leadership

▫ Trustworthiness

▫ Courage

▫ Communication skills or effective communication

Even more interesting, I learned during my interviews with them that many of these mindsets were in fact strategically developed. That is why I believe that anyone who is highly motivated to succeed can develop the top advisor mindset.

The first step is to examine the mindset traits and compare them to yourself. Don't be discouraged if you only share some of these traits: Look at the gaps as areas of your mindset that can be enhanced. All that is required is the desire to become better and the willingness to invest the time and energy to improve.

Professionalism Is the Gold Standard

Our top advisors understand that image is important, and that the more affluent investors are, the higher their expectations of their advisors in every facet of their lives. And when it comes to their finances, investors want to feel that they are dealing with true professionals who take their career and clients' assets very seriously. That's why presenting an image of professionalism is very important.

All of our top advisors dress like professionals every day. In many cases, they look like their clients and have invested time and money to create that image. They often look like a senior executive or partner in a large law firm. Their image reflects their serious attitude toward money.

Their professionalism is carried down to their staff members as well. The top advisor office is well organized, nicely decorated, and conservative in appearance. Their associates have been well trained to greet clients and prospects in a very professional way. When visitors come they are treated graciously. Phone calls are promptly answered in a professional way. And, like the advisors they work for, associates adopt attire that is both conservative and professional.

While you may not have the same resources, office space, and personnel as the top advisors, taking your professional image and presence seriously is very important. These top advisors all started with very modest means, but they always took their professional image seriously and did everything within reason to project the image of a top professional.

Showing Confidence

Confidence is a quality that is often developed over time. The majority of our top advisors started their businesses at a young age, and while they had high goals for themselves, they didn't have the experience required to portray a high level of confidence. However, they all recognized that to acquire the most affluent clients, a sense of confidence was critical.

Confidence in yourself, and in your professional financial advice, is intrinsic to the nature of the financial planning and advising industry. In most cases, advisors aren't selling specific financial products: They are selling themselves. The top advisors don't pitch new products they are offering to potential clients; instead, they try to position *their* wealth management process and *their* level of confidence in themselves. The goal is to get new clients to believe in you so that they will listen to your advice and ultimately follow your recommendations.

Portraying a high level of confidence is important in any field, yet being a professional financial advisor is different from most occupations. Financial investments usually contain some element of risk, and therefore they inherently have uncertain outcomes. As advisors, we know that risk can be offset to some degree by a good investment process, but the overall outcome still remains uncertain. Because of this uncertainty, investors expect their financial advisors to have a high degree of confidence in themselves, as well as their investment process. Think of it this way: Interviewing a financial advisor is like interviewing a surgeon before a major operation. For many affluent investors, their financial health is just as important as their medical health and they require the same confidence from their financial advisor as they would from their physician. Before submitting yourself to a potential life-threatening surgery, you not only want to know that your surgeon has experience and credentials, but that he has complete confidence in his own skills as well as the outcome of the operation.

Our top advisors never hesitate to show a great deal of confidence in their ability to manage their clients' investments. However, they invariably choose to portray the quiet confidence of a true professional, not the false braggadocio of an incompetent. Listening to them describe how they invested money, I wanted to transfer my own account to any one of them because of how confident they were in their investment strategies. Their success rate in closing with prospective clients is very high because the prospects always feel they are in the presence of at "true professional" who has the confidence to help them achieve their objectives.

Another element of confidence our advisors share is their willingness to turn away business if they did not perceive the right "fit" between themselves and particular new prospects. Turning down business is one of the highest forms of demonstrating confidence: It shows that these advisors were not willing to compromise their business model just to take on more clients.

HOW TO BECOME MORE CONFIDENT

Developing a high level of confidence in yourself and your business strategies can be accelerated when you become comfortable with your investment process and you begin to see positive results. At the same time, you also need to develop a comfort level with the uncertainty that inherently exists in this business. The right process will produce good results over time, but short-term volatility will always exist and must be put in proper perspective. Your process of investing is more important than the specific investments you choose. Developing an investment process that works will give you the confidence you need to convey your strategy. Then, when clients follow your well-thought-out process, you know that over the long term they can reach reasonable objectives.

If you want to become a top advisor, you must accept the fact that you will be working with individuals who are more affluent than yourself. Being respectful but also being your own person, and all the while demonstrating the quiet confidence of a true professional, is an essential quality. For example, when Sam was a young financial advisor he joined a prestigious country club. Sam often found himself in the company of many of his city's most prominent citizens, most of whom were older. He always showed a great deal of respect for their success and position. He was a good listener, and because of his excellent interpersonal skills he became friends with many of these highly successful individuals, despite the age difference. Over time Sam developed these personal relationships into some of his best clients. Without the right combination of confidence and respect, Sam would not have been able to develop these personal relationships that eventually led to business.

HOW TO BECOME A CONFIDENT LEADER

Clients expect leadership from top advisors, just as they would from any professional they hire. Leadership skills are one of the hallmarks of a highly successful financial advisor. The mindset qualities of leadership and confidence are very similar. Affluent clients expect leadership and confidence. Confidence comes from preparation, experience, and a commitment to professional development. Leadership is transferring that confidence into action. Because investments have an uncertain outcome, clients need to be "led" to take action.

Our top advisors were not necessary born leaders, but acquired this skill over time. They are the leaders of their teams. They are the ones who provide the vision for the team and oversee its execution. Not all the top advisors wanted the leadership responsibilities or even felt they were good leaders, but they recognized it was their responsibility and as a result provided it.

When the stakes are high and the outcome is uncertain, being a leader is required. The top advisors are strong leaders to both their clients and team members. They tell their clients how to invest their assets and never hesitate about how that should be done. When they make investment recommendations to their clients, they expect the client to follow their recommendations. If a client consistently doesn't follow their recommendations, our top advisors often divest themselves of that client.

Taking Risks

Courage in the financial services business means the willingness to take yourself out of your comfort zone so that you can have the opportunity to bring in more affluent clients, all the while knowing that you might face certain rejection. Marketing and the ability to deal with rejection are essential to your ultimate success, and without the courage to face these challenges, a lucrative practice is difficult to build.

One of the important qualities of successful people in this business is that they have the drive to complete necessary but difficult activities.

It's not easier for successful people to do difficult tasks, but they have the ability to make themselves do whatever is necessary to get the job done. For example, in financial services, rejection often occurs because many affluent prospects already have an existing relationship with another financial institution and/or another advisor. To convert a prospect to a client you must disrupt an existing relationship. Affluent prospects can be reluctant to change advisors because of the importance of their investments and the uncertain outcome. It takes time to gain the confidence of a new prospect, so be prepared to face rejection numerous times before the prospect becomes a client.

Our advisors demonstrated their courage by marketing themselves to individuals that were affluent. It took a great deal of courage and confidence to approach affluent prospects who in most cases had high expectations of their financial advisors and were more sophisticated than less affluent individuals. These top advisors would not allow themselves to be intimidated by wealthy individuals and larger institutions. They kept raising the stakes by working with more and more affluent individuals, and as the sophistication of their prospects increased, they remained willing to move out of their comfort zone. Some of their more risky strategies that have paid off include:

> ❏ *Cold Calling.* Anne was a financial planning specialist before she was a financial advisor. She never made a marketing contact prior to becoming a financial advisor, but that didn't stop her from calling high-powered CEOs from day one. Rob moved to America from his native country of India after college and started to work with a major investment firm. He became a master cold caller and established a million-dollar practice by his sixth year in the business. Despite their multimillion-dollar practices, both Anne and Rob still make cold calls every week to wealthy individuals in their target markets. Mike, too, started his financial career right out of

business school and started making cold calls to some of the wealthiest individuals in his market.

❑ *Creating a Niche.* David worked in a rural state where finding affluent individuals was a challenge. Early in his career he developed a strategy of contacting institutions and competing for their retirement plans. He did not let his lack of experience keep him from competing for institutional clients; he simply worked hard at becoming a consulting services expert so that he could compete in this more sophisticated market.

❑ *Having a New Market Focus.* Dana moved her practice to another part of the country and developed a new marketing strategy focusing on nonprofit organizations. Within six years she had doubled her assets, bringing in hundreds of millions of dollars.

Taking on the Competition

Being a competitor is another mindset quality that all our top advisors have. They are not obsessed by competition, but they have a healthy respect for it. They like to win, and many of them also enjoy competitive activities outside of work.

A competitive trait can have some negative connotations, as you begin to imagine the "win at all costs" mindset. However, this is not the kind of competitor I am referring to. Our top advisors want to do well among their peers. They care about their careers and take a high level of pride in being a top professional. Every one of the top advisors I worked with cared about the scorecard. They could tell you their firm's ranking not only in the current year, but in past years, too, and where they expected to be ranked in the future. This is the kind of healthy competition that the top advisors have. In many cases the improvement in the scorecard is an important reward, albeit intangible.

For example, several of the top advisors were consistently ranked in the top-10 nationally within their firm. They take a great deal of pride in that ranking and could at any given time rattle off the names of the other top-10 advisors and tell you exactly how they were ranked.

Setting Goals

One of my favorite quotes about the financial services business is, "You can't manage anything you don't measure." This philosophy is shared by our top advisors as they set clear goals and worked toward achieving them, even if these goals have changed throughout their careers. In many cases these advisors would smile as they shared how modest their initial goals were compared to the success level they eventually reached. In my observations, successful advisors set goals, less successful advisors do not.

It is also important to track your progress and hold yourself accountable to your plan. At any given time I could ask these top advisors what their goals were and they could tell me what their goals were and exactly where they stood in terms of achieving them. Not all objectives were always met, but they were always set. When I asked one top advisor about his goals, he pulled out a beat-up notebook and showed me how he had recorded every year's goals and his weekly progress toward those goals for the last 20 years.

Setting clear goals is a "mindset" quality that is an easy one for any motivated advisor to attain. The first step is to set a reasonable goal for both the long term and the short term. Long-term goals of five years or more can be broken down into smaller, annual goals. Once the annual goal for that year is determined, it should be broken down into weekly goals that add up to the annual goal.

Some of the most important goals to set are:

- *Business Goals*. How much business is expected to be completed over the next 12 months, including the total number and percentage change?

- *Asset Goals*. How many new assets can be expected to be brought in over the next 12 months, including percentage change?

☐ *New Affluent Household Goals.* How many new affluent households can be expected to be brought in over the next 12 months?

☐ *Client Retention Goals.* The affluent client retention rate you can expect to have over the next 12 months expressed as a percentage (the higher the better).

☐ *Prospect Pipeline Goals.* How many qualified prospects in your pipeline—this is a leading indicator of business.

During the interviews, all of our top advisors could tell me, without hesitation, how much business they had done in the last 12 months, how many new affluent households they brought in, and the total value of the assets brought in. In short, they all kept score.

Being a Visionary

A vision is the long-term direction and business plan that you develop as the means to achieve your goals. All of our top advisors have a clear vision about their business and where they want it to go. Interestingly, most of the top advisors did not recognize that they had a clear vision when they first started. "My visions were to do the right things for clients, stay on the phone, and do business," says Sam.

For many, it seems that survival was the first step in the process, but over time a more sophisticated, well-thought-out vision emerged. In many cases this vision changed dramatically through their careers. One of the top advisors admitted that he had reinvented himself almost completely throughout his career. Another top advisor talked about the five stages of his career and how each stage contributed to a higher level of business. Another top advisor, Dana, talked about how she started almost by accident in the retirement planning area and aspired to be the best in it, later shifting her vision to the nonprofit world.

Visualize what you want your business to look like now and in the future. It doesn't have to be a perfect vision, and it will probably change. But if you start with one, you are doing more than most financial advisors in our business.

Developing a Strong Work Ethic

The top advisors all have a strong work ethic. They started their careers working extremely hard, and while they may not work as many hours now as they used to, on average they still work 50 hours a week. It was the hard work in the beginning of their career that distinguished them from their peers and contributed to their early success. While most of the top advisors did not have the clear vision in the beginning of how to build a million-dollar practice, they all knew that hard work was the first necessary step.

It was a combination of a strong desire to succeed and a fear of failure that provided the commitment to work long hours from the beginning. These advisors recognized that they couldn't control the markets or whether people would do business with them. But they could control their own efforts and hours worked. Their early success came from sheer effort, mostly making a large number of cold calls. They all worked nights and weekends and spent whatever time was necessary to build a successful practice. Many of them used their spouses to help develop marketing lists and other administrative work. John, who today does more than $7 million in business, spent his first year in business consistently working 70 to 80 hours a week.

Hard work is something every advisor is capable of. If you are motivated to take your business to the next level, then you must also be willing to work hard. Having high goals is not enough; it's the daily execution of the right activities that will determine their successful outcomes. However, long hours are not enough, either; you need to focus your work hours on the right activities in order to achieve success. These activities include spending time with clients and prospects, meaning that you are continuously developing relationships with affluent investors. If you are not willing to spend at least 50 percent of your day interacting with affluent clients and prospective clients, then you aren't spending your time on the right activities.

Passion and Energy

Passion fuels energy, and as a result these mindset qualities go together. Many of our top advisors look at their long careers in financial services as a gift. They all enjoy their work and believe that they are making a meaningful difference in the lives of their clients. Most important, they were grateful that they were making more money than they believed possible. Despite their financial success, none of the top advisors talked about early retirement or burnout. Rather, their positive feelings gave them a continued and palpable passion for work. Even when they work long hours, our top advisors have a passion for the job that is related to a high level of enjoyment. They spend time entertaining clients and prospects and are involved in outside organizations that are a combination of work and fun.

In an industry known for high stress and burnout, they have maintained a high level of passion for the business. That passion and energy not only results in a strong work ethic, but also a high level of productivity. It's hard to say what comes first, the energy or passion, but both of these mindset qualities feed on one another.

Communication Is Key

Our top advisors are all very effective communicators. Their skills include presentation skills as well as the ability to comfortably carry on one-on-one communication between themselves and their clients. They all have the ability to take complex investment ideas and strategies and relate them to their clients in a simple and effective manner. They also communicate their professional competence without appearing to be arrogant or overly confident. They speak with a combination of confidence and empathy, and have created a powerful communication style. These advisors can adapt their style to fit the individuals they are interacting with. They are able to do this by being good listeners and observers of others.

The hallmark of each of these top advisors' communication skills is their ability to relate to affluent individuals, project confidence, and engender trust. Their collective effective communication style is based on a genuine concern about the financial well-being and personal lives of their clients. Caring comes first and foremost with being a good listener. These advisors are focused on all aspects of the client relationship, not just the client investments. They care deeply about their clients, and that sincere interest comes across when they communicate with them. They are effective in social situations because they are focused on people, are good listeners, and have the ability to make people feel comfortable.

Our top advisors are also capable of making formal presentations to individuals and groups, and there is a wide range of experience and ability in their skills. Approximately half of the top advisors have developed world-class "pitch books," the formal, written presentations they use with prospects, and have invested a lot of time and energy in developing them. The objective of a pitch book is to share, in a condensed but professional way, what the client experience is like and how the investment process works. For example, John told me that his business is built on the belief that "the best presentation wins." He knows that if he has the opportunity to make a formal presentation with his pitch book, in almost all cases he wins the business.

The other half rely on their interpersonal skills with less formal presentations. The lesson is that the formal presentation skills, while important, are not as critical as the one-on-one communication skills. Presenting skills are important but not nearly as important as being able to listen. Active listening enables advisors to tailor their approach to the needs of the client or prospect.

Affluent investors can sense who the advisor cares more about: the client or themselves. If you can learn to focus on client needs and become attentive to the personal side of the relationship by being a good listener, you will be on the right track to becoming a great communicator.

Being Perceived as "Trustworthy"

Most people have an innate sense of whether someone is trustworthy. Our top advisors recognize that developing a relationship of trust is their highest priority. As a result, these men and women always put their clients ahead of themselves. They never let their business ambitions get ahead of doing the right thing for them. Despite their long tenure, the compliance records of the top advisors are virtually spotless. They are principled individuals and have demonstrated those principles from the beginning of their careers. They also fundamentally believe in a long-term orientation. That is, they recognize that they are in their careers for the long term and are willing to make less money initially to develop a long-term relationship of trust. They know there is tremendous leverage in having satisfied clients, because satisfied clients provide referrals and are willing to bring more money in once the relationship of trust is created. That confidence also enables the advisor to provide leadership. When clients trust their advisor, they will follow their advisor's guidance. A relationship built on trust takes time to earn, but once established, it's priceless.

You must put the interests of the clients above your own. This business of money can bring in both temptation and rationalization, which must be resisted. To become a top advisor, a long-term orientation must be adopted whereby you recognize that even if less money is made in the short term, you will be rewarded in the long term by loyal clients, which can't be valued more.

In the end, it isn't just one of these mindset qualities that defines a top advisor; it is the combination of all of them. By incorporating these lessons into your attitude, you'll find that all of the other lessons you will be introduced to, from this point forward, will be easier to follow.

2

The "Leverage of Size" Principle

A SUCCESSFUL financial services practice is better measured by the asset size of each client's investment portfolio rather than the total number of clients. It doesn't take more time to invest $1 million than it takes to invest $100,000, but the fees generated on the million dollars are obviously higher. This discovery of the "leverage of size" came to our top advisors at different times in their careers, but eventually they all came to the same conclusion: Working with fewer, more affluent clients was essential for them to build the multimillion-dollar practices that they all achieved.

There are, however, consequences for working with more affluent individuals. First, the expectations of the quality of your service increase. Clients expect good performance at a reasonable price, a strong relationship with their advisor, and Ritz-Carlton service. Affluent individuals are constantly targeted by financial services companies, so these consumers know what your competition is offering at all times. What's more, they have high expectations and will shop around for the best, because of the many choices they have. To provide exceptional service, you'll quickly find that there is a limit to the number of clients you can work with. In fact, the more affluent investors you attract, the fewer relationships you will be able to handle. The highest-producing top advisors have the lowest number of total client relationships (between 50 and 100), but their minimum client sizes were the highest.

For example, Greg, one of our top advisors, was mentored early in his career to create relationships with the most affluent client base in his area. He started with a handful of clients and continued working with this model throughout his career. Today, Greg works with some of the most affluent individuals in one of the nation's largest markets.

John, another of our top advisors, also told me that providing great service is the key to maintaining fewer, better relationships. "When I had 600 clients, every time one of them called, I had to tell my assistant that I would have to call them back. I was always on the phone with someone else. That's not providing good service. Today, I would much rather open six or eight very affluent relationships than the 50 new smaller relationships that I used to open every year." John's advice is to limit the number of total relationships to less than a hundred and to only prospect for new relationships that are bigger than your average size. John's team works with 80 total relationships, and he works directly with 40 of those relationships. Those 80 relationships represent more than $1 billion in total assets.

Joseph currently does $7 million in business, but he was intimidated by big money early in his career. When I asked him what he would have done differently, he immediately answered, "I would have gone after bigger pools of money earlier. I was intimidated and wasn't confident I could handle large pools of money. My comfort zone was with $500K accounts, and I was intimidated about going for a $5 million account. But looking back, I found the guy with $5 million had the same goals as the guy with $500K."

Dana Organized Her Way to Fewer, Better Clients

For the first three years of her business career, Dana cold-called her way to success, opening many small accounts that put her in the top of her peer group. But Dana wanted more. In an effort to improve her business, she asked a top advisor in her region if he could mentor her. Dana's first question was to see how this advisor organized his desk. Dana wasn't interested in seeing how neat he was. Instead, she wanted to learn what his real priorities were. In his left hand drawer, he had 20 file folders that were his top-20 clients. On the right side of his desk were his top stock picks and the research that backed up each one of them. This setup taught Dana that this top advisor was always prepared if any of his top-20 clients called. This information also made Dana realize that as much as she was encouraged to bring in large numbers of clients, she had to focus on a smaller group of clients that were really going to bring in the business for her.

Dana formulated a second revelation from yet another top advisor she interviewed. This top advisor taught her that she needed to increase the potential of each client. Instead of asking for $10,000 to invest, she needed to ask for $100,000. That meant that Dana had to have clients capable of giving her at least $100,000. She began to weed through her book of business, giving away her smaller relationships. Then she started to aggressively pursue larger prospects. This insight and change of business model ultimately led Dana to first a million-dollar and later a multimillion-dollar practice.

David Created New Products to Land Bigger Clients

David started in a smaller market, but quickly recognized that it was going to be too challenging to open enough affluent relationships to reach the level of success he wanted to obtain. Early in his career he decided to specialize in retirement plans. He learned that the size of each individual investor didn't matter as long as there were a large number of them that had their assets pooled together. David developed the expertise and credentials to market and compete successfully for the largest retirement and pension plans. This strategy paid off, because he became the most successful advisor in his market.

Rob's Career Kept Changing with His Client Base

Rob describes the evolution of his career in five different stages, with each stage leading to clients and prospects with more assets.

"The first three years I opened a lot of small accounts mostly from cold calling, building my book up to 500 accounts. I found I had reached a plateau by having to service these accounts all the time.

"The second stage came when I discovered another way to do business: the managed money and fee-based approach linked with retirement plans. At the time I focused my marketing efforts on retirement plans for small business owners, physicians, and attorneys. These types of investments offered a higher level of minimums. I recognized that larger pools of money could be found in small retirement and pension plans, and that those retirement plans were interested in the fee-based managed money platform: I could charge clients a fee based on the assets they had invested, as opposed to charging for each transaction. This second stage took my practice to $1 million, but I realized that to go beyond a million, I needed larger pools of money to manage."

To become more competitive for larger retirement and pension plans, Rob needed to become a true investment consultant, which required a higher level of expertise. He needed to learn how to develop policy statements, the formal statements of how assets will be invested, as well as create more sophisticated asset allocations through the careful analysis of the class of assets in each portfolio. He also needed better access to the backgrounds, track records, and investment styles of the money managers he was outsourcing to, as well as their performance records.

As his expertise grew so did his ability to market effectively to larger pension and retirement plans and high-net-worth individuals in the $5 million to $10 million range. Rob spent more than 10 years at the third stage of his career, which took him to the $3 million level. He was managing more than $300 million in assets/money to generate that level of business.

The fourth stage of his career started when he became a charter member in a national organization focused on entrepreneurs in the technology industry. Rob's brother was one of the successful entrepreneurs, and he made introductions into the organization. Rob's timing was good as the technology boom was taking off in the late 1990s. He was being introduced to "money-in-motion opportunities"—the movement of money from one source to another. In his case, Rob focused on the sale of businesses to larger companies, and he leveraged his investment consulting expertise to help members of the organization who had sold their businesses. This was a classic money-in-motion scenario, and Rob was able to capitalize on it through his involvement, leadership, and expertise in this organization. His practice moved forward and became national in scope, with the majority of his new relationships valued at more than $10 million.

Rob looks at the fifth stage of his career as getting referrals within his firm for partnering opportunities. Today, Rob has an $7 million practice. He works with 78 client relationships; their total assets are

$1.4 billion. His goal now is to bring in at least four highly affluent new clients a year, and he has averaged $100 million of new assets every year for the past five years.

Money in Motion is a common marketing theme for many of the top advisors because it gives the advisor an immediate opportunity to provide advice on how best to manage money that comes as the result of a liquidity event. The ability to identify money-in-motion opportunities also paid off for another one of our top advisors, Mike, who from the beginning was trained by his company to compete in this high-net-worth space. He started calling money-in-motion prospects with at least $1 million in potential assets from his first day as a financial advisor. As a result of his focus—and the development of the expertise of working with larger relationships—Mike built a multimillion-dollar practice within five years.

Implementing Lesson #2

The first step is to recognize that to grow your business by adding increasingly affluent clients, you must have both the time to proactively prospect and the business practices in place that allow the ability to retain and attract wealthy clients. Providing outstanding service and having the time to market your service will naturally limit the number of total client relationships you will be able to work with. Every one of our top advisors came to this same conclusion. They found that if the affluence of their client base increased, they could generate more business with fewer clients.

Every client that receives proactive contact and world-class service requires at least 10 hours of your time a year. This time is spent on a combination of monthly contacts, quarterly reviews, an annual planning session, and client events. Because you have limited time, you need to make sure that every minute of your day counts toward moving into the top advisor category. As top advisor John points out, "Every client belongs on someone's A-list." This means every client should be important to the advisor that client works with.

If you already have 100 client relationships or less, then your objective should not be to increase the number of clients, but to continually upgrade that investor base by replacing smaller, less productive clients with larger, more productive ones.

If you already have much more than 100 client relationships, I suggest you group your existing clients into three different categories, or tiers.

Tier 1 should include the 20 percent of clients that account for 80 percent of your business. The 80/20 rule has absolutely been validated by my 20+ years as a manager in the financial services industry. Time and again, I have seen real evidence that 20 percent of clients represented 80 percent of an advisor's business.

Tier 2 should be those existing clients with the potential to become Tier 1 clients over the next 12 months. They should be contacted at the same frequency as Tier 1 clients, which is monthly. After 12 months, Tier 2 clients should be reevaluated based on actual business consummated as well as their potential. Then, decide which ones to keep and which ones to divest. The objective over time is to move the Tier 2 clients to Tier 1, with the total number of Tier 1 clients not exceeding 100.

Tier 3 clients are those remaining that don't meet the other criteria. There are different views on what to do with Tier 3 clients. One view is to pass them along to another advisor who will treat them as Tier 1s; this approach is strongly recommended. The other view is to simply not make any proactive contact with Tier 3 clients, and only respond to their occasional service requests—the less preferred method. If their service needs are high and continue to be low revenue producing, they should be divested.

There are certainly some smaller Tier 3 clients that should be kept for a variety of reasons. They might be related to larger clients, for example, or they have always been good referral sources or are in some personal relationship with you. An important caveat regarding the focus on bigger relationships is that, in the beginning, you will require smaller relationships for your own financial survival. With only three exceptions, the top advisors all started their careers opening small accounts. Once they reached a critical mass they began the tiering process, which in some cases was years after they started.

Many of their smaller accounts developed over time and eventually became multimillion-dollar relationships. These smaller accounts became larger in one of two ways: They were high potential relationships that were developed and nurtured over time, or the top advisor discovered that these clients held assets away from them and eventually the entire portfolio was taken over through the wealth-management process, which you'll learn about later.

Redefining Your Business

After your initial weeding, look over the two tiers of clients you still have. The total number of customer relationships that an advisor can make regular proactive contact with—and commit to providing world-class service for—should be about 100 accounts. It can be more or less, depending on the size of your team and the support that can be provided.

All financial advisors, no matter where they are in their career, should set a minimum for their clients. This minimum should be greater than the average size of your existing Tier 1 clients. My recommendation is that even a new advisor set $100K as a minimum. If the relationships are smaller than that and have no potential for growth, you will be spending too much time developing prospect relationships that aren't big enough to justify the effort spent. Economically, these smaller, low-potential relationships are better served at the right price point by the highly discounted firms that don't require the time-intensive work of the full-service advisory firms.

Systematically raising that minimum is one of the key strategies to growing your practice over time. An experienced advisor should aim for at least $250K as a minimum investment. As the business grows, continue to elevate that minimum number. For example, Taylor Glover never stopped raising his minimum through his 30-year career before reaching his $100 million minimum.

Once the minimum level of assets is determined, use this number as a screening tool for prospective clients. When you approach clients or other potential influencers for referrals, make them aware of your business strategy: that you are looking specifically for clients that meet your minimum investment requirements. The majority of our top advisors indicated that they made exceptions to their minimums if they felt that a new client relationship had a higher potential. For example, Ross was very specific that he would take on a smaller, younger relationship that had high potential over a retired prospect that might have more money but no potential to grow.

The following dialogue is an example of how to ask a client for a referral while referencing a minimum size:

> "I am very proud of the wealth-management process and service we provide our clients, and I am confident that if affluent investors were aware of our offering they would benefit from working with us. Our challenge is finding qualified investors who would benefit from working with us. I wanted to ask you if anyone came to mind that we could help. Specifically, we have found that we can help investors who have at least $250K to invest and who are going through a change of circumstance in their lives, like a job change, promotion, moving into the area, going through a divorce, or a recent loss of a spouse. Does anyone like that come to mind?"

Ross Sets a Floor for His New Clients

Like many of our top advisors, Ross started his business cold-calling anyone who would invest with him, but as his business grew he recognized the leverage of relationship size. Today, he is very selective about the new relationships he brings into his practice.

He explains his logic with this example: "Say I meet someone on the golf course and I know they have a high net worth, and they'll ask me to invest just $50,000. I would say I'm not interested, because that's not what my business model is about. I am not about doing just a single transaction; I want the entire relationship." Ross also says, "I will take on a person with high potential but less money over someone who has the same amount of money but not much potential beyond what they invest with us any day of the week." Today, Ross and his partner have a total of 120 relationships, all over $1 million, with 50 of them over $5 million and 25 over $10 million.

Forecasting for Growth

Another important factor in choosing which clients to work with goes beyond their asset size. You also need to consider the minimum amount of business that they will actually do over a 12-month period. If a client does not do a minimum level of business, no matter how big they are, I would recommend that you divest them. As an advisor motivated to growing your practice, you simply can't afford to waste your time with clients that don't follow your recommendations and are not "on board" with your business model.

In many cases the reason clients don't meet set business minimums is that a distinct business strategy has not been developed for them. Each client in your practice deserves the time spent on developing and executing an appropriate business strategy. A second reason that clients don't meet a minimal level of business, even if they have significant assets, is that they are not exposed to enough financial products and investment choices. By taking a holistic approach to wealth management, you can expand your business beyond portfolio management to all the client's financial needs, including liability management, estate planning, asset protection, banking needs, and retirement planning. If you can offer all of these services, you can ensure that the minimum level of business is met.

Continuing the Discovery Process

One of the most valuable insights that I gained from our top advisors is that the easiest assets to obtain are those from existing clients. A relationship of trust between you and the client already exists, which is much different from starting fresh with a prospective client. Many advisors assume that they have all of their clients' investable assets, so they don't bother to orchestrate a thorough discovery process regarding each existing relationship. However, if the right discovery process is done, most advisors will be amazed at how many of their client's assets are undisclosed. Once these assets are discovered, a strategy can be developed and executed to bring these assets into your business.

Most of our top advisors were fanatics about knowing everything they could about their clients, including their held-away assets. For example, Dana would use the following conversation prompt to discover such assets:

> "I don't need to manage all your money, I just need to understand where it is so that I can determine what I'm going to do for you and how it will interact with all your other assets."

Dana told me that once she knew there was money held elsewhere, she would become very aggressive. "I will call with ideas and say I know you have money at XYZ Financial, and what do you think about moving that to me, so we can buy my recommendation," she told me. She shared one example of a client with a large bond portfolio. She offered to give him a free analysis on all his bonds, including those he held elsewhere, and he agreed. He loved the analysis, and as a result, Dana brought in millions of dollars of bonds. Every time she meets with this client during their quarterly review, she brings up assets held away by asking, "How are you doing on the other accounts?" Talk about them—in Dana's case, they represent a significant amount of the new business she brings in every year.

Jack told me that many of his top-20 clients started off as smaller clients who had assets scattered around between other investment firms and banks. Over time, these clients found that they enjoyed working with Jack and the service he provided. With his encouragement, they eventually moved many of their held-away assets to Jack.

Affluent Clients Require Time

Affluent clients are influenced by a high level of service and the frequency of proactive contact that they require. If each client is contacted proactively once a month, and three of those contacts are quarterly reviews and one is an annual review, then a minimum of 10 hours annually of proactive contact is required for each relationship. With 100 client relationships, this works out to a minimum of 1,000 hours a year of proactive advisor contact, which alone represents half of an experienced advisor's working time. Affluent clients also require a very high level of service in the areas of problem resolution, responsiveness, professionalism, and follow-up. Advisors who want to attract bigger client relationships must provide this kind of service.

One of the powerful marketing lessons I learned from our top advisors is that to attract increasingly affluent investors you must be in a position to interact in nonbusiness settings with them. This means that you have to become part of their community. Many of our top advisors believed that their most effective marketing occurred when they were where the affluent people were, and at any moment they were prepared to make the transition from the personal interest to a business meeting. The techniques for engaging clients in nonbusiness settings are described in great detail in Chapter 6.

For most advisors, it would be economically challenging at the beginning of their careers to make the financial commitments required to be part of an affluent community. It is relatively inexpensive and easy to join alumni organizations, the chamber of commerce, religious groups, or civic organizations. Yet as the target prospects increase in value, so does the price of admission to be part of their community. Making donations to nonprofit organizations for board membership, joining private clubs, and travel and entertainment expenses all require financial resources and major time commitments.

One Hundred Is the Magic Number

Once you attain 100 affluent client relationships, you can start focusing on increasing your income by growing the size of each of these relationships. Over time, you can set new and higher minimums for new clients, but don't increase your total number of clients past 100. As I indicated earlier in the chapter, exceptions to 100 can be made, but these should be the exceptions, not the rule.

I have often told advisors that in reaching the million-dollar level, the most important factor in determining the ability to reach the next level, a multimillion-dollar practice, is being able to raise the affluence of the clients you are working with. This takes courage, confidence, and patience: all aspects of the top advisor mindset. Courage is required because working with increasingly wealthy people and larger pools of money will take you out of your comfort zone, but growth never occurs when you are comfortable. Confidence is required because affluent investors want to work with investment professionals who show that they believe in themselves and their investment processes. Finally, patience must be tested in the proactive pursuit of highly affluent investors.

Professional Development

THE DESIRE TO develop professionally and grow intellectually is part of the DNA of each of our top advisors. From the beginning of their careers, they all had an insatiable appetite to improve themselves. Their motivation was primarily driven by the desire to succeed: They all realized that as their expertise grew, so would their business. They shared a genuine interest in the financial markets and a desire to translate their professional growth into doing a better job of investing for their clients.

The professional growth success principle ties directly with the previous "size matters" success principle. As your larger client relationships grow, you will see that more affluent clients have higher expectations of their advisor. These investors have many choices when it comes to selecting an advisor to invest with, and they all want the best. Growing professionally is a prerequisite to showing that you have what it takes to work with the affluent investor, as the expectations and demands of the wealthy are always high.

Many times in my career, I have been asked what separates the good advisors from the great ones. My response is always the same: "The good become great by always getting better, never being satisfied, and continually growing professionally." Top advisor Jack once told me, "I don't think you have to be an authority on every subject, but you've got to have enough curiosity and interest to keep up with changing trends, changing products, changing ways of doing business. You have to be open and willing to listen to new ideas. You don't have to be the smartest guy, but you have to be well read and know where to go to get the knowledge you need."

Greg adds to this point when giving advice to other advisors aspiring to a multimillion-dollar practice: "Increase your knowledge, develop a high level of expertise, and never stop growing professionally." I have found that all of our top advisors are voracious readers, committed to staying abreast of current events as it relates to their business. They know that their clients expect them to interpret and understand what is going on in the markets. Staying current and being well-read keeps them prepared to enter into any conversation with their clients.

Joseph describes the evolution of his business as the primary reason for his need to stay informed and grow intellectually. "I have grown with my clients," he says, "and when bigger opportunities came, I needed to develop the ability to handle those bigger opportunities without falling on my face." His learning curve grew to satisfy the demands of his clients needing more sophisticated advice.

The Evolution

With only one exception, each of the top advisors began their careers knowing very little about investing, the markets, or how to make more money for their clients. They were drawn to the business for different reasons. But most of them were driven by the excitement of the financial markets and the opportunity to create success based entirely on their own efforts. For example, Dana had a natural intellectual curiosity as a former teacher and MBA student. She told me, "I wanted to be excellent, and I was a sponge for every kind of information I could get. I had incredible energy to be a student of the markets and to learn new products. I used that knowledge in situations for social prospecting—not to pontificate at a cocktail party, but to be able to show intelligence when interesting conversations came up at one. To have the depth of knowledge to discuss interest rates or the markets left people thinking, 'Wow, this person really knows what she's doing.'"

As a rookie in the business, Dana realized quickly that she was not going to learn much from the other rookies she was sitting with. She shared with me the following story: "I was sitting in the bull pen around ten guys that were all starting when I did, and I realized I wasn't going to get the knowledge I needed just through osmosis. So I set up meetings with senior and successful advisors that were part of my office and region." Dana gives credit for her success to the insights that she received from those early meetings with successful, senior advisors.

Mike realized that he had a steep learning curve when he entered the business. "I worked very hard living a one-dimensional life during the early years of my career," he says. "I made a real commitment to learning as much as I could about the investment process and about our trade and craft. I realized the importance of expanding my knowledge and growing professionally, so I was able to have the confidence required to market to my highly affluent target market."

Professional Growth Sets David Apart

David realized from the beginning that his success would be dependent on his knowledge and professional development. He told me that he studied for the Series 7 exam, the test required to get licensed to sell securities, to acquire the knowledge he needed, not just to pass the test.

David gives credit for the progression of his career to his continued quest for more knowledge and professional development. "I always thought knowledge was what you needed to get to the next level. Knowledge gives you confidence, and confidence is required when working with affluent individuals and large pools of money," he says. According to David, throughout his career he was willing to invest in himself intellectually and he made sacrifices: "Early in my career I would always be willing to spend time when I needed it to learn a new subject, at the expense of a golf game."

David also believes that professional development quickly separates the top advisors from the rest. He believes that the top advisors are in most cases the most knowledgeable. According to David, there is no way to reach superstar status as an advisor without knowledge: "If you show me a top advisor, you can rest assured they know a lot about the business."

The Bar Is High

It's not enough just to learn this business when you start out. Your knowledge has to continuously grow, especially as the sophistication of your clients increases. Rob cites an example that illustrates this point with a story: "I recently met with one of my most affluent clients, and she started to ask me some questions about the current financial crisis. She wanted to know my worldview, including my opinion, on whether we were going into a serious recession. I realized that she was looking to me to find out for herself what was going on in the economy. To answer her, I knew that I had to come up with a thoughtful view that I could substantiate. You cannot wing significant questions from significant investors." And that's what he did. In the end, his thoughtful understanding of the markets and his ability to express a thoughtful view to his clients is what bonds them to him.

Greg makes the same point in a different way. "With very large client relationships," he says, "you will be asked to provide well-informed answers around significant questions about investment decisions. For example, a large client sold their business and ended up with a large, concentrated position. He wanted to know what their options were. Should they collar the position? Participate in exchange funds? Sell shares under the 144 rule [selling restricted and controlled securities]? These clients expect you to have the expertise and knowledge to provide them with their options and guide them."

Professionalism vs. Salesmanship

I'm often asked by new advisors if I could recommend a book or a course on salesmanship. My response has always been that our industry has moved beyond salesmanship and that professional competence is the most valuable commodity they could offer their clients and prospective clients. In the 1980s and even the early 1990s, the financial services industry was more product-oriented, and salesmanship was a required skill to have. However, in the twenty-first century, the most successful advisors are those who have a high level of expertise in comprehensive planning that translates to solving their clients' investments needs and helping them achieve their financial objectives. This shift in the business translates to a shift in client expectations. Today, clients are not looking for salespeople; they are looking for the most competent professional financial advisors they can find.

Rob speaks for all the top advisors when he makes the following point: "Unless the transition from pitching a product to being an interpreter of the economy and financial markets is made, advisors will never reach their potential. As a financial advisor, you cannot delegate your responsibility to understand the world around you. I'd be exceptionally skeptical that, by simply selling a product, you could consistently do big numbers. To consistently do big numbers you have to invest enough time and effort to be able to continuously interpret the economic world around you."

Rob believes the level of expertise and professional development that financial advisors need is much greater than some pundits espouse. In particular, Rob takes exception to comments made by a well-known author and financial services speaker. Rob maintains, "I would take the counterview to the statement that once you figure out how to sell mutual funds you can grow your business to the sky." Rob's point is that if you are just a mutual fund salesperson, you are going to plateau quickly.

Being "a shepherd of assets" is an expression that Rob uses that accurately reflects the top advisor's views of the most important aspect of this occupation. As an advisor, your clients entrust you with the oversight of their financial health and reaching their objectives. Each of the top advisors takes that responsibility very seriously and recognizes that being on top of their game is essential to being a good shepherd of their clients' assets.

Making Time for Personal Growth

There is an inherent conflict between spending time doing business and professional development. The industry compensates advisors only when they do business, so there is no short-term incentive to spend time on professional development. However, if an advisor doesn't spend time on professional development, it will be hard to create a competitive advantage or to effectively market to the higher affluent market segment.

Rob shares how he makes this balance work. "I spend a fair amount of time on keeping my professional interests alive. It is essential that you be passionate about your ability to keep track of what's happening in the economy and the world. That extra effort is natural for me because of my passion and interest in investing. I am seeking answers for myself [as much] as I'm seeking them for my clients, and my clients know that. The bottom line is that if you're passionate about it, you will find the time to learn." As Rob says, the best in the business enjoy professional development and view it in many ways like a hobby. They spend many hours outside the normal working day in pursuit of becoming better at their job, and they get a high level of satisfaction and enjoyment in that pursuit.

However, professional development should never be an excuse not to spend time developing client and prospect relationships. All of our top advisors spend the majority of their time with clients and prospects, and they would never put professional development ahead of the relationship side of their business. The reality is that both must be done to reach top advisor status.

Another incentive for advisors to invest time and effort in their professional development is the retention of their existing and most profitable clients. Our top advisors know that having a good relationship with their clients is not enough: They must continually be the best in their market. Rob expands on this point, saying, "You may be an ace marketer and have the ability to close deals with new prospects, but if you don't do a good job of investing their money, then you will bring clients in the front door and lose just as much money through the back door. I've seen a number of advisors do exactly that. My belief is the majority of advisors who don't reach a million-dollar business can blame their failure on the fact that they haven't made the necessary commitment to acquiring the expertise needed to effectively manage money."

Our top advisors typically work 50-hour weeks. If four to five hours a day are spent with clients, prospects, and making marketing contacts, that leaves plenty of time for professional development. The client and marketing time should always be the first priority, and with good time management techniques (discussed in Chapter 13), this work can be accomplished by lunchtime on most days.

Implementing Lesson #3

The development of this success principle starts with having a genuine intellectual curiosity about the financial markets and how they relate to the current world that we live in. An important step in this process is acquiring a professional designation. The most common designations are the Certified Financial Planner (CFP) and Certified Investment Management Analyst (CIMA). There are other specific designations that reflect a high level of expertise in specific financial areas, including Certified Retirement Planner (CRPC), Chartered Life Underwriter (CLU) for insurance and estate planning, and Chartered Financial Analyst (CFA) for investment analysts.

The advantage of a professional designation is that it conveys to people the level of expertise that is required to practice in the financial services industry. It is also an important way to distinguish yourself from the competition. For example, to achieve the CFP designation, you must pass a rigorous exam that requires the understanding of 100 different topics on integrated financial planning. Less than 10 percent of all registered advisors have the CFP designation. Several of the top advisors actually have both the CFP and CIMA; this combination demonstrates to their clients and prospective clients an extremely high commitment to their profession.

Advisors who make the commitment to improve their professional growth through a professional designation have a major competitive advantage. It gives their prospective clients the opportunity to make an objective comparison between an advisor with a professional designation and one without one. Your designation is a powerful marketing statement to any prospective client. It implicitly states that you have made a significant commitment to your career by achieving these professional designations. Conversely, when you meet prospective clients, the first question you can ask of them is, "Has your current advisor made the same commitment to his or her expertise?"

Joining a Professional Organization

Another step that can be taken for professional development is join-ing a professional organization like the Investment Management Consultants Association (IMCA). IMCA is an ethical and trustwor-thy conduit to cutting-edge investment strategies. The association provides a multitude of resources and continuing education oppor-tunities. This is exactly the kind of organization that can contribute to professional growth.

Additionally, you can keep informed by joining a peer group of other highly motivated successful advisors. Usually these peer groups are informal and developed by the advisors themselves. The objective is to share best practices with each other to help all mem-bers of the peer group improve. Ross puts it well by stating, "The knowledge you get from talking to people who are the best in the industry will separate you from the rest."

I recommend identifying the most successful advisors that do business the way you would like to and visiting them. Some of the most effective training I offered people who worked with me was to do an office visit with a top advisor. Having a chance to watch them in action, meet their team, and ask them questions provided the experience that up-and-coming advisors respond to best. These office visits usually involve travel and may mean compensating the interviewed advisor for his time. However, the rewards have always been worth the price.

Knowing the Ins and Outs of Your Niche

In many cases, successful advisors have identified a target niche and developed the expertise required to serve it. As you develop experience, you will also develop an expertise. Finding the answers to questions that your clients don't know is critical to attaining a body of knowledge. You can acquire the ongoing knowledge required to be an expert in a specialization from books, articles, and experts. Read industry publications and attend the association meetings of targeted professional groups. Two excellent sources are available for finding associations and trade magazines that are relevant to your niche:

- AssociationExecs.com lists more than 17,000 associations.
- Tradepub.com lists more than 1,000 trade magazines.

Because David's target market is retirement and pension plans, he knows that the expertise he has developed separates him from his competition. In David's words, "I knew that I wanted to work in an area where there was a barrier to entry. In my case, there was a mountain to climb in terms of knowledge. Most advisors aren't willing to spend the time necessary to develop the required expertise. This fact alone reduces the amount of competitors and gives you greater confidence to show your clients that you're the right choice."

Keeping Abreast of the Market and Financial Theory

Reading books and articles that provide a historical perspective on the markets and proven investment practices will further contribute to your professional development. Some books I recommend are *The Intelligent Investor* by Benjamin Graham, *Stocks for the Long Term* by Jeremy Siegel, and *Buffett: The Making of an American Capitalist* by Roger Lowenstein. I also recommend reading reports and the many daily and weekly financial periodicals that will keep you well informed of current events in the world and how they relate to the investment markets, such as *The Wall Street Journal, The Economist, Forbes, Investor's Business Daily,* and *BusinessWeek.*

Interestingly, professional development was not a success principle that I had focused on when I started writing this book. But I realized that it was an important ingredient to building a successful practice when several of our top advisors convinced me that it was not only important but essential to building a multimillion-dollar practice. As my interviews continued, I realized that all of our top advisors were "students of the business" and were never satisfied with their level of knowledge.

I also learned that many of our advisors acted as teachers to their clients. They transcended beyond just providing information; they were able to take the mystery out of the markets and successful portfolio management. They taught their clients how to become successful investors in order to reach their financial goals.

In my opinion, mastery is only achieved when you know a subject matter so well that you are able to teach it to someone else. Our top advisors are masters, yet they never stop in their quest to become even better. Subsequently, they are continuously evolving and growing, and attracting even more affluent investors.

4

Specialization

SPECIALIZATION IS tied closely to professional development. That's because a specialty emerges through the insights and expertise gained through a commitment to learning and honing your craft. The combination of these two success principles is powerful, creating a top financial advisor who can be an expert in one particular niche market or type of investor.

Each of our top advisors has developed an area of specialization. Two of them entered into this business with an expertise in a particular segment of the market, and then combined their knowledge to create a new business based on that expertise. The rest of our advisors started as generalists but realized that the most efficient and effective way to build a practice was to narrow their focus and develop an expertise within a niche market.

In most cases, their specialization was determined by the type of clients with whom they were most successful, or whether they had clients in the same industry. Often their specialization changed during their career, primarily driven by the constant search for more affluent investors. A few of the advisors interviewed for this book knew from the beginning the niches they wanted to focus on, but the majority evolved into their specialization as their business grew.

Ross tells his story this way: "I was a generalist for a long time, and I found that I had to be an expert in a thousand things. I discovered you don't become an expert doing a thousand things one time. You become an expert doing one thing a thousand times." Ross believes that in order to be a top advisor you have to specialize. His specialty is senior executives and business owners who have sold or plan to sell their businesses. This process is referred to as "money in motion."

John started out as a generalist as well, but evolved into a specialist. Today he limits his clients to those having assets of $10 million or more. As he reflects on his 30 years in the business, he comments, "I use this analogy with my prospects. If I knew that I needed a heart transplant, why would I want anyone other than a heart surgeon?"

Why Specialization Works

The specialization success principle works for a number of reasons. First, being a specialist separates the expert from the generalists, and most people prefer to work with an expert. I've found that affluent investors want to work with an advisor who specializes in working with investors that have similar circumstances as themselves. Doctors want to work with an advisor who specializes in doctors, just as executives want an advisor who understands their unique needs. One of the most important questions an advisor can be asked is: "Why should I work with you?" The answer is always: "Because I specialize in working with people like you."

Also, by specializing, you can commit your time for professional development in a specific direction. Rather than trying to be an expert in many areas, you can go "deep and narrow" and continue to develop a high level of expertise. This makes you even more attractive to a niche market and raises the barrier of entry for competitors.

In addition, as you successfully penetrate a niche market, you will build a reputation as an expert within that market. As your reputation grows, it will become easier to get referrals within that niche. You will also be able to determine the *centers of influence* within your niche. This refers to those individuals who have achieved a high level of respect within their industry. If you can develop a relationship with these individuals, not only can they provide you with valuable insights about their industry they can also provide you with referrals. The combination of a good reputation and endorsements from centers of influence will generate new business.

Best of all, when you develop specializations within a niche you become known as "an insider." As an insider, you should read the publications in your area or areas of expertise, go to the necessary association meetings, know the players, and speak their language. These habits reinforce the connection among prospective clients within your specialization. Being able to provide references to successful people within your niche market is yet another marketing opportunity for your business.

The Benefits of Casting a Small Net

David began in a relatively small market and initially struggled to find enough individual affluent investors to build a large practice. So he focused on retirement plans, reasoning that even though his prospects weren't making a lot of money individually, if they were grouped together he would be prospecting a very large account. David realized that to be able to compete for these assets he would have to develop a high level of expertise and focus on retirement plans. He joined the Investment Management Consultants Association (IMCA) and obtained the Certified Investment Management Analyst (CIMA) professional designation. With these credentials behind him, he felt that he had developed the skill set and knowledge necessary to work with large pools of institutional money. He says, "I found myself in my market as one of the first adopters of the institutional investment process, based on modern portfolio theory. I was able to distinguish myself from the pack because I could explain a process and methodology of how pension funds should be invested. In the beginning my prospects had little experience with policy statements, asset allocation study, and monitoring performance. But I had the expertise in these areas, and my knowledge was appreciated."

Ross started out as a generalist and built a good practice with individual investors. After a while, he brought on a junior partner who believed that executives of public companies and business owners selling their companies would be good target markets. Together they expanded these markets to include money in motion and developed the expertise needed to be competitive. In Ross's words, "We look for money in motion. If you find some great privately held company you get in there, because it's probably not going to be privately held for long. I focus on which businesses are getting sold, [which people] are acquiring businesses, and where wealth is being passed along. All of these are [examples of] new money that is not somewhere else, and we want to be there first. In my experience, this has been the best place to find gigantic clients."

Since Ross's practice became more specialized, the team's business has more than doubled in the past six years. Ross is still able to use his past experience with investing money for individuals, but he is much more targeted and specialized in what individuals he approaches and how he approaches them. As a rule, before he and his partner go to any meeting, they research the companies fully. For example, he once approached the CEO and CFO of an oil company that was going public. "We impressed them with our knowledge of restricted stock and liquidity," he said, "and when they saw how good we were, they invited us to look at their other money."

William specializes in working with retirement plans and pre-retirees. He says, "My first niche was architects and engineers. I chose them because they had enough money for retirement plans; more important, they worked in small offices and answered their own phones, so I could get through to them directly."

William found that seminars were an effective way to get in front of pre-retirees: "If I could find a situation where a reduction of employees was occurring, I would volunteer to host a pre-retirement seminar. Once I was doing an IRA rollover seminar and it happened that a client invited someone that worked in a different branch of the same company about an hour away. Afterward he called me and asked if I would do a meeting for his branch in their conference room, which I did. He called back again and asked if I would be willing to give my talk on a larger scale. And so we cobbled together some flyers of what we were doing and I dropped them off at his office. He actually distributed the announcement for me. I rented [space at] a local hotel and 50 people showed up. And then for the next four months I would meet with people from that company, doing proposals and opening accounts."

Mike used a different approach. At the start of his career he was hired by a firm that specialized in the high-net-worth market. Early on he learned the expertise that was required to effectively approach this specialized market: "Some people claim that they are really good at trust and estate planning, or really good at alternative investments, or really good at managing the investment process. We specialize in pulling it all together in a cohesive way so that those individual parts are working together to achieve a single goal for the families that we advise. I believe our ability to integrate the different aspects of investment management is unique."

The Specialties of Our Top Advisors

Many of our top advisors have more than one specialty, although those specialties are often connected. They include:

- Successful owners of privately held businesses
- Professional referral sources (CPAs, attorneys)
- Executives
- Nonprofit organizations
- Pension and retirement plans
- Corporate services such as stock options, 401(k) plans, and deferred compensation
- Entrepreneurs
- Professionals, including physicians and attorneys
- Retirees/pre-retirees (IRA rollovers)
- Private wealth (individuals who have investable assets of $10 million-plus)

Implementing Lesson #4

It's interesting to note that for our top advisors, it wasn't so important how they found their specialization or what their niche markets were, but rather that their success came from the intrinsic power of specialization: the very positive impact that it had on developing their top advisor practice.

Try to identify potential niche markets in your area that you can pursue. David suggests that you look for voids in markets where there are not as many competitors. First, you'll need to understand the demographics of your target area and match yourself up with what's needed within that space. Once the opportunities are identified, you will then need to ask yourself, "What skill sets are really needed to serve the market?" Finally, you will need to acquire those skill sets and determine how to best serve that market.

Niche markets should include markets with both short- and long-term lead times. Niche markets with shorter lead times might include business owners, executives, and your own personal contacts. Longer lead time niche markets are those that will take at least a year of work for any potential clients to materialize; in this category are specialties such as nonprofit organizations and developing a professional referral network. I recommend that all advisors have at least one short lead time niche market and one with longer-term lead time, because while you are waiting for the longer lead time niche market to produce results, you'll have a short-term niche market that will provide new affluent clients and assets.

Your level of specialization will get deeper as a particular niche market emerges as one you have success with. Over time, a superficial expertise will grow deeper, which will give you the confidence it takes to become a real expert. For example, Dana told me that four months into her business, a senior advisor at her company left and they distributed his accounts. As always, the rookies got the smaller accounts and she was assigned several accounts, one of them a $2,000 IRA that belonged to a doctor. According to Dana:

"I called the doctor and asked if I could meet him to discuss his IRA account. He told me that he was too busy, because he was in the process of revamping his entire pension plan. He then asked if my firm offers retirement plans. I told him that we did, and I immediately went to my manager, because I had no idea about retirement plans. He gave me a couple books to read about defined benefit and contribution plans. I went home that weekend and read up on our firm's offerings. My manager joined me at the presentation and it turned out to be a $700K profit-sharing plan with five doctors, and we got the business. One by one, each of those doctors became personal clients, and they're still clients today, 25 years later.

"This was a huge break and it gave me enormous confidence. The relationship grew, and all the while I was developing a specialization in retirement plans with other doctors. I really developed quite a big business not only with medical professionals, but with any small, private company with people that offered retirement plans. Best of all, it was like an ongoing annuity, because every year they're going to invest more money."

Dana later relocated her practice and changed her specialization to take her business to the next level. She developed a new expertise in philanthropic services and used that specialty to leverage her involvement in nonprofit organizations and working with endowment funds. Through this change she doubled her business and assets in six years.

Narrowing Your Focus to One or Two Niches

Continue to serve each of your different niches by obtaining some level of expertise, identifying qualified individuals in these niche markets, and contacting them, as well as gaining the necessary experience that will contribute to your expertise. Over time, one or two niche markets will emerge and you can start to go deep and narrow, developing the expertise required to be a real specialist.

The only exception to this approach is if you came into the business with the high level of expertise necessary to attract affluent investors. For example, Anne started her career in financial planning, and after an entry-level job she was promoted to develop financial plans for individuals worth more than $10 million. She covered Silicon Valley in California as well as Washington State during the tech boom years, spending three-and-a-half weeks a month on an airplane and developing an expertise in mergers, acquisitions, pre- and post-IPOs, and high-net-worth planning strategies. After several years, she decided it was time to settle down in one location and become a financial advisor.

Leaving the comforts of her planning job and starting as a new financial advisor was a challenge, she says: "I realized that in my new market I had more expertise than anyone else, so I went after a targeted group of people. I cold-called them and told them about my expertise. I informed them that they were at a point in their careers that they needed to work with an expert and suggested we meet. If the prospects said they were working with someone else, I gave them a list of questions to ask their current advisor and told them that I would call them back in a week to share my answers. Usually the prospect would compare the answers and then decide to meet with me. As I opened new accounts I would ask for referrals, and usually I got them as well."

Anne's vision, expertise, and specialization paid off and she reached the million-dollar level by her second year in the business. In her seventh year, her team did $5.5 million and her share was $4 million. She manages $1.3 billion in assets, which means she has brought in more than $150 million of new assets a year. Her early success is the best I have ever seen in my 30 years in the business and is a testimony to how powerful specialization can be.

Analyzing Your Client Base

For advisors with more than two years of experience and a solid base of clients, if an area of specialization is not obvious, I suggest that you do a market analysis of your business. Go back to your list of Tier 1 clients, which should include the 20 percent of clients that account for 80 percent of your business. (If necessary, go back to Chapter 2 for advice on how to group your existing clients into three different categories.) Use this list to help you determine what type of occupations—including retirees—represent the highest percentage of your best clients. In almost all cases, this category will make clear what niche market you are most effective with, which will in turn point to the one that will be the basis for your specialization.

Don't Forget to Market

Having a specific expertise often isn't enough: You have to be willing to market aggressively to targeted prospects. One mistake many new advisors make is spending too much time attempting to develop a high level of expertise before they begin to market themselves. In most cases experience is the best teacher, and while developing some initial level of expertise is important, it shouldn't be done at the exclusion of marketing and getting in front of affluent investors. For example, Anne's expertise combined with her ability to communicate and willingness to market is what led to her success.

If you have confidence and the expertise to back it up, then getting as much exposure as possible within your targeted niche markets will generate prospects and eventually business. There are two primary ways for you to leverage your expertise within a niche market. The first way is to immerse yourself in your targeted niche market by reading that market's publications, joining the industry associations, and developing relationships with the centers of influence. The best first step is to enlist your current clients in your niche market to help you by serving as your "marketing board of directors." They will be able to help you form excellent ideas concerning how to most effectively approach targeted prospects within your niche market, and they can make suggestions as to what associations to belong to, what trade magazines to read, and help identify the niche market's centers of influence. The board can also provide suggestions on what type of marketing approach would be most appealing to them, and this information will give you a good idea what would appeal to others in that market. Use your marketing board to vet the names of qualified prospects, asking for permission to let you mention their name as a reference.

The second way is to simply contact qualified individuals directly. For example, Anne contacted potential investors in her target market by sharing her expertise and offering to help them in a way that no one else in the market could. A combination of both ways would be especially effective in niche marketing.

Continuing Your Professional Development

Once the process of identifying your specialization is complete, your professional development process can continue as well. The objective is to increase your level of expertise so that there will be few competitors that can cross over the barrier of entry and compete with you in your new area of specialization.

In addition to obtaining knowledge by immersing yourself into your niche market and visiting with other experts, I also recommend attending association meetings and taking advantage of all networking opportunities. You can offer to do a presentation on investment strategy, planning, or retirement that is relevant to that specific industry. The opportunity to mix with other professionals with potential clients at these meetings will contribute to building your reputation as an industry insider.

At the same time, you should be reading the local and national periodicals and newsletters that cater to your new market. Periodicals usually feature the most successful individuals within a targeted group and focus on the current issues facing that particular industry. Writing articles for a trade magazine is another way to establish yourself as an expert in that particular market.

When I was a new advisor, I made the decision to focus on smaller towns that were within an hour's drive of my office (this became my niche market). My logic was that there would be less competition, and as a new advisor it would be easier for me to get in front of qualified prospects. In the beginning I stumbled into this strategy, but as I kept at it I got better and better, and once I established a following in one small town I moved to another one. I always found that I was successful in a shorter time in the next subsequent town.

Without even realizing it, I had become an expert in marketing to affluent investors in smaller communities. I learned firsthand the power of specialization. Not all of your clients need to be in your specialization, but if you aspire to greatness in this business, you must develop an area of expertise.

5

Relationship Focus

FINANCIAL HEALTH and security are among the highest priorities people have in life, which is why understanding the psychology of investing is so critical. No matter how intelligent or logical the individual, fear and greed will always affect investment decisions. These emotions can wreak havoc on one's financial investments, which is why so many wealthy individuals choose to work with a professional financial advisor.

Our top advisors all realize the importance of understanding their client's psyche, and they take this knowledge into account when developing investment plans. They also understand that building trusting relationships with investors and prospects is essential to building a successful financial services practice. They know their clients like they know their best friends and in many cases it's because their clients are among their best friends.

Once a good partnership with clients is established, all good things come: more assets, referrals, and the buy-in to your recommendations. All top advisors share this success principle, and aspiring top advisors should make relationship building with affluent investors one of their highest priorities. Unlike most goods and services, asset management has virtually no guaranteed outcome and is completely intangible. Yet because of its relative importance, a financial advisor is often chosen on a gut instinct that is connected to a high level of trust. In fact, the product that financial advisors are really selling is "trust." That's why the relationship between the client and the advisor is critical to your success. Top advisor John explains that a financial advisor is "the person that they go to with any kind of question, financial or otherwise, to help them in their overall personal and financial needs. It's almost like [being] a financial psychiatrist. A lot of times I'm dealing with issues with children, next generation, their hopes, dreams, and fears. It's a whole series of things that go beyond investing."

Mike describes the partnership in the following way: "They don't view me as a vendor, and I don't view them as a customer. I view myself as having a very significant moral obligation to deliver the best I can, and to represent their interests well. I refer to it as a sacred trust. They realize the competence and work that goes into representing their best interests, and I think they value that. I realize that we would not be in our position if it weren't for the wonderful relationships that we are fortunate to have with our clients. It's all about the trust they have in us that we always put their interests first."

Our top advisors learned early in their careers that investing time in developing relationships with their clients and prospects was the best investment they could make. This relationship focus becomes increasingly important as the wealth of their client investors increases. The highly affluent have so many choices that professional competence is not enough to seal the deal: In fact, many of our top advisors found that the relationship was more important to landing new prospects than their expertise. However, a trusting relationship is also easy to lose. Mike observes that "the connection between me and my clients is based on a very fragile relationship. One misstep, one misjudgment, one self-centered movement putting your interests over your client's, and decades of hard work can go out the door."

Honesty Is Still the Best Policy

Twenty-five years into her career, Dana is more committed than ever to the relationship-building process. She shares a recent conversation that she had with a very large client: "He said to me, you know we work with you because we like what you bring to the table, but more importantly, we think you are honest with us."

Dana knows that the appreciation of honesty stems from having a strong relationship with people. "It comes from the way they see you interact with other people," she says. "It comes from the way they see you treat your kids. The more experiences you have with people, the more confidence they have in you. If you're a good person it's going to come through, but you have to develop a relationship first so that people can see beyond just the business."

When she meets with prospective clients, Dana follows the same routine she has honed over the past 25 years. She describes her early prospecting contacts as follows: "I never lead with a product; my goal is to get people to talk. It is more of an open discussion of what they need." Dana's objective is to have longer conversations to gather as much information about her prospects as possible. She keeps notes on the conversations, including anything personal they discussed. Then, when she follows up with prospects, she asks about those personal things.

Dana is convinced that building a relationship and gaining trust has been an important component for her success. She talks about the dynamic between relationship building and trust: "I developed a sense of trust with people. They felt a sense of trust in me because I understood what made them tick. I asked them a lot of questions about themselves and I'd listen carefully. I developed an understanding about what their 'hot buttons' were. I showed an incredible amount of empathy and concern for them that was genuine. What I really did was develop a relationship. When it came down to whatever we were going to do from an investment standpoint, it was a lay-up by the time it came to that, because I had already developed a relationship."

Implementing Lesson #5

The first step in building a relationship with affluent individuals is to be where they are and do what they do. Sam recognized early in his career that he needed to be where the wealthy people were, doing what wealthy people did. As he explains, "Rich people play golf, so I learned to be a good golfer. I joined a country club, so I could play golf with the right people. I also knew that in my area, rich guys like to fly-fish, so I became an expert fly-fisher. Rich guys also like to hunt birds, so you have to know not only how to bird hunt, but [you have to] have the right guns, be a good shot, and know the etiquette. I made my activities outside of work align with my potential clients."

David believes that you must get into the right settings where you can meet affluent people and then see who you relate to best. Those individuals will become great clients, so spend your time creating and building relationships with those people. "Some people will lead immediately with their investment knowledge and try to forge a business relationship. I try to forge a personal relationship first," David says. "It's great to have a wonderful relationship with someone and then allow them to find out you're a very knowledgeable person about the investment business."

Understanding the Motives
of Prospects and Your Clients

Jack strongly believes that understanding and responding to his client's personal needs can be just as important as meeting their business needs when it comes to building relationships. Jack has a number of elderly clients, and he knows that they often need more than financial advice. "They want friendship; they want to know that someone cares about them, because often their children have moved away. We provide extra attention and time because it makes a real difference to them," Jack says.

Ross is fanatical about knowing everything he can about his clients and prospects. He knows where his best clients went to college, what church they go to, what their outside interests are, and what their kids are interested in. Ross's philosophy of knowledge allows him to leverage this client information into a more productive business relationship. He told me the following story: "Once I met a CEO client at his office. While I was waiting for him I looked around and saw a picture of his daughter teeing off and underneath the picture it says 'Colorado State High School Golf Championship.' Right then I found my conversation starter: something I can talk to him about; personal information that will form the basis for our relationship. From that one photo I could tell that we had a common interest—golf."

Learning to Forget About E-Mail

Mike shares a basic communications lesson he learned the hard way: "I learned not to use e-mail as a primary communication tool with my affluent clients, because it is an impersonal way to deal with somebody. You can't develop a real relationship because much of the nuance of interpersonal communication is lost. In this business, it is important to understand how people feel about things. Not just the words they say, but their tone—how they react, and how to customize your message to them.

"When I first started to do business with one client he professed to be a very, very busy guy," Mike says. "He stated that his preferred means of communication was e-mail. At his request I communicated with him solely by e-mail, and so rather than just picking up the phone and having a conversation, or even responding to his e-mail questions with a personal call, I indulged his request. When he transferred his account, I realized that I had made a fundamental mistake."

Investing in Relationship-Building Activities

The top advisors all recognized that an important component of building a relationship with their clients and prospects is to invest time with them beyond the business. For example, Jack has always been a good athlete. He runs with a large group every Saturday morning, as he has for 30 years. The members of the group are not the fastest runners in town; in fact, they are committed more to fitness than speed. However, many of them are very successful professionals. "There was a guy that ran with our group every Saturday morning, who knew I was in the investment business. He would ask me about the market when we were running," Jack says. "I never solicited him in any way, and about four months later, he invited me to his house to meet his wife and go over his portfolio. He meets with me and decides to consolidate all his assets with me, and all of a sudden we're bringing in a really nice pool of assets. I never knew he had that kind of money, and there will be more coming because there's a fair amount of real estate. But that's not the end of the story: He then referred me to a friend of his in the town he used to live in, and that friend has turned into an affluent client."

Entertaining or hosting dinners are good ways to connect with prospects. Anne entertains by taking one client and his or her spouse out for dinner. John often hosts dinner parties at his house, typically inviting 12 guests. The dinners are catered affairs with very nice food and wine. John usually invites two existing client couples along with two couples that are friends, and two prospective client couples. These are all people he knows, and the conversation is never centered on business. The point is relationship building. Having been invited to several of these dinners myself as John's manager, I can attest to the quality and effectiveness of these intimate dinners. His wife is a wonderful hostess; everyone has the opportunity to get to know John on a personal level during these dinners.

Dana hosts dinner parties at her house and invites both her clients and prospective clients. "I make the dinners a wonderful way to get to know people. I hire a private chef. I have eight people at the dinner table and have a killer [menu] with fabulous wines, and [it becomes an occasion to] bring together people I think would be compatible. They get to know my husband and kids and get to know me a little better. They see me in my house; I make it warm, set the table beautifully. I make it a lovely evening, but I don't make it stuffy."

David organizes a ski trip every year to Beaver Creek, Colorado, for his best clients and prospects. He enjoys putting people with similar interests together for a weekend and finds that "people love it and love you for organizing it." Ross organizes fishing trips with his best clients and asks them to bring people they think Ross should meet. He says, "If I can take a guy fishing and have a good day, he's mine forever. I book two days at a fancy trout lodge, and then call a good client and invite him for either day. I choose a lodge that's hard to get into, where the fish are known to be monsters. Then I ask the client to bring someone he thinks I should know; the right clients understand what I'm looking for. I'll take along my camera and shoot a picture of my client and his guest, holding a big fish. Later I'll give the client and his guest the photo in a nice frame so that every time they see it, they remember the great day we had together."

You might be wondering how much you can afford to spend on these relationship-building activities. What exactly is the price of entry to gain access to wealthy investors? As a less experienced advisor, realistically you will start smaller, and as your success progresses so will your ability to develop a retained earnings budget that you can invest in developing relationships with more affluent investors. Remember, fun activities don't always have to cost a lot of money. In the beginning, the time spent with prospects and clients is more important than how much money you spend. Less expensive activities are available, which include buying tickets to sporting events or arranging visits to fun but inexpensive restaurants, college alumni events, and art or museum exhibits.

Prioritizing Your Time

How advisors spend their time is a true reflection of what's most important to them. For our top advisors, the majority of their time is spent on the relationship side of the business (75 percent), leaving 25 percent of their time for handling administrative issues, research, reading, proposal preparations, e-mail review, meetings, and operational tasks. One-third of that 75 percent is time spent with prospective clients. This allocation of time reflects the importance of relationship building.

The only way an advisor can build a relationship is to invest the time in one. Start every relationship by getting to know the prospect, not just from an investment point of view, but also personally. As John says, most people don't care how much you know until they know how much you care. Asks questions, listen carefully; pay attention to their office, including the pictures, awards, and diplomas they display. The details all contribute to a better understanding of what makes the person tick.

Bridging Friendship and Business

When a good relationship is built, the opportunity to discuss business will occur. In most cases it will be brought up by a prospect, and when it is, you need to be ready with a transition line that can bridge the personal relationship to business. That way, you can start to transition the discussion from personal to business matters on your terms, when you are completely ready.

For example, if a prospective client should ask (and they all will) what you think of the market, you should be prepared for a transition line that might sound like the following:

> "You know, as a wealth manager, I really take a long-term view on the markets, but I have access to one of the best investment strategists in the business. He writes a weekly commentary about the conditions of the markets, and I would be happy to put you on my e-mail list to receive his reports. Would you like me to do that for you?"

The prospect will usually agree. You can follow up later by saying, "What did you think of the investment reports I've been sending you? I would enjoy having the opportunity to discuss our investment process with you. Would you like to meet for coffee, and I'll share my investment approach?" In this way, you are in charge of the conversation: You are directing the relationship.

The transition from a personal to a business relationship will be successful if, through your actions, you can raise questions in the prospect's mind that they would be better off working with you rather than whoever they are currently using. This conversation can occur during the initial business meeting, regardless if you are simply having a talk over a cup of coffee or having a more formal appointment at the prospect's place of work or your office. However, ongoing follow-up builds the case further. The challenge is for you to position yourself as a strong second choice. Eventually, as the relationship develops, you can create doubt about their current advisor, and through your actions you can make a case that the client is better off with you. By using this strategy, you'll find that the client's assets will in many cases be transferred to you.

There are no shortcuts to effective relationship building, but it is the best time that can be invested in growing a successful financial advisor practice. The relationship between a financial advisor and a client is one of the most important professional relationships. I've found that the best advisors are the ones who take this relationship seriously and invest their time and energy into more than just the business aspect of the relationship. As I've mentioned before, investing money for other individuals must be done in the context of understanding their emotions, current life situation, and what's most important to them. Our top advisors all shared the belief that making a positive difference in the lives of their clients is what they enjoyed most about this business, even in down markets. To really make a difference, you need to put in the time to build the relationships at the beginning, and then continue to invest your time in really understanding what your clients need and expect. By becoming part of their lives, you will transcend service-provider status to become a trusted partner.

LESSON SIX
Marketing Best Practices

MARKETING IS A requirement for any successful business, including one in the financial services industry. Our top advisors never stop marketing. The desire and willingness to grow their practice has become part of their professional DNA, and they often market without thinking about it—it's a natural process for them. In my observations, it is one of the most important differentiating factors between top advisors and those that are less successful. In many ways the specific marketing tactics are less important than having the ability to find ways to develop relationships with affluent investors.

Because they put themselves in the position to interact with affluent individuals all the time, our top advisors continually have the opportunity to market. Whether they use the traditional or indirect marketing techniques, the goal for financial advisors is always to build more, new lucrative relationships with affluent investors.

Ross explains how important marketing is when he says, "The number-one factor in my success is marketing. Your marketing strategy is your ticket to bringing in new money. Whether it's cold calling, seminars, referrals, or networking, you always need to be bringing in new money."

This chapter describes the marketing tactics that our top advisors have used to build their multimillion-dollar practices. However, as important as the individual tactics are, it is more important to have the motivation to carry them through. All types of marketing involve the potential for rejection. If you market, you must be willing to face potential rejection.

There are two reasons most advisors don't market. The first is that they don't know how to do it effectively, and the other is because they are not willing to face the inevitable rejection that comes with marketing. The willingness to market must come from within you. The simplest way to describe the motivation dynamics of this business is that your desire to grow your practice must be greater than your fear of rejection. To implement the marketing success principle, you must have the motivation to use appropriate tactics.

Rejection is an inevitable part of this business, especially when you focus on the most affluent investors. Remember, wealthy investors are likely to already have another financial advisor or financial institution. For you to be successful, you must disrupt that current relationship. Even if your prospect is not completely satisfied with her existing financial relationship, it is a known quantity. Working with you is unknown. Because of the importance of their investments and the uncertainty of investment outcome, it will take an "act of faith" for these investors to make a switch. This should not deter you from trying, as long as you are prepared to live with the fact that rejection is part of the marketing process.

For newer advisors, it can take up to ten marketing contacts, using a variety of tactics (including seminars, a professional referral network, Rolodex marketing, cold calling, networking, adopt-a-town tactics, and event marketing) to result in a single face-to-face appointment. If you have a good follow-up process, you can expect to close about 25 percent of your prospects within 12 months. More experienced advisors will meet prospects mostly through existing personal relationships or referrals, and their ability to get an initial appointment is very high.

Getting Past Rejection

The average million dollar producer in the industry opens approximately 3 new million dollar plus relationships a year. The new affluent client goal I encourage motivated financial advisors to set is 10 a year. The point of these statistics is that you don't have to "win" a lot to "win" big in our industry if you are focused on the affluent investors. This is a low-percentage/high-pay-off industry and you should keep that in mind as you proactively market. The right attitude is to focus on the positive and not on the inevitable rejection. Remember, part of the top advisor mindset is confidence and believing that what you offer is valuable. This is the only way to approach marketing in financial services. If someone rejects your offer to help, it is their loss, not yours. Realize, too, that like most things in life, the more you do it, the better you get, and the less rejection you'll have to face as you learn to position yourself and your services better.

Cold Calling: A Beginner's Marketing Strategy

Our top advisors all started without a book of business and had few connections. They were not members of a team. Every one of them spent their early years making cold calls. This marketing technique got them in front of their target prospects and gave them a feeling of control. While they couldn't control whether people did business with them, they could control how they spent their daily activities. These top advisors didn't know any other way and didn't want to wait to get started.

None of them would say cold calling was easy or even efficient, but for all them it worked, and like everything else they got better with experience. Their desire to succeed (or fear of failure) overcame the fear of rejection. The objective was to get a face-to-face appointment, which is the first step in building a relationship with prospects.

For example, Joseph started in 1982 with one goal: to make 175 contacts with new prospects every week. He focused on making appointments to open new accounts and IRAs. In his first year he opened 50 accounts with new clients and 111 new IRA accounts. Joseph would call business owners, individuals that lived on "nice streets" in his community, and doctors. He started to call doctors whose last names began with the letter *H* because he thought that no one else would start cold-calling in the middle of the alphabet. Today, his clients still include 20 doctors whose last names begin with "H." He admits his methods were not very sophisticated, but what he lacked in sophistication he made up for in hard work.

Dana describes her early year's cold-calling method as follows: "I did a lot of cold calling. I would work until 9:00 p.m. four nights a week, Monday through Thursday, setting up appointments to meet with people. Once I got the appointment, I almost always got the account. I believe I was successful because I developed a sense of trust with people. I asked them a lot of questions about themselves and I'd listen carefully. I began to understand what made them tick and got a good feeling about what their hot buttons were. I showed an incredible amount of empathy and concern for them, which was genuine. They perceived me as being different than the average person cold-calling them, because I made an investment in them."

Mike made cold calls from the beginning and describes his early years in the following way: "It was very hard, very difficult. There was a lot of rejection, but that was the only way I knew how to do it. I focused on liquidity events, where there were decisions that had to be made. I didn't come from a wealthy family and I didn't know wealthy people, so I had to start from scratch. The reason I got into this business was because my success would be a function of my own efforts, what I did, not waiting for somebody to do it for me, so I made cold calls."

Sam started his career cold-calling, working from eight in the morning to nine at night, four days a week, and 8:00 a.m. to 5:00 p.m. on Fridays. He called outlying areas outside the major city where he worked. He tried to set up his appointments one day a week. Once he got the appointment, his objectives were to get an account open, do a good job, and try to get them to transfer all their assets to him over time. He kept following that strategy for his first five years in the business.

Ross's cold-call strategy consisted of being able to articulate his firm's competitive advantages and to convey to prospects why they should do business with him. The following is an example of his approach:

> "Hello, Mr./Ms. Jones, this is Ross and I'm a financial advisor at XYZ Financial. I'm calling to see if you're dealing with our company. [Most of the time the answer was no.] Is that because we haven't called or because you invest elsewhere? Mr. /Ms. Jones, I'll get right to the point. If I could provide you with a better return at a lower cost than you are currently getting, would you have an interest in speaking with me?"

Rob admits that cold-calling was not easy, but he got better the more he did it. He focused on getting appointments because he believed that he was most effective "in person." He used this marketing approach for his first three years. He noticed that many of his friends that started with him stopped prospecting after their first year and, as a result, plateaued early in their careers. In contrast, Rob built his book up to 500 clients.

William started by getting a business directory and cold-calling architects and engineers. His logic was that these professionals had enough money so that they would need retirement plans. He also found that most of them worked in small offices and answered their own phones, so he could get through to them.

Cold calling's greatest nemesis is voicemail. The most effective way to deal with the inevitable is to leave several messages introducing yourself and the purpose of your call. It is important to provide a strong value statement in the message to set the stage for when you finally reach the prospect. Once you have left four messages without a returned call, then you have one last shot. The final voicemail should be simply your contact number and an invitation for them to return your call if they are interested.

Top Marketing Techniques

Our top advisors chose between many effective marketing strategies, finding success with all of them. Their techniques have evolved, but they've never stopped using them. There are five primary ways in which they market:

- Client Referrals

- Professional Referral Network

- Niche Marketing

- Event Marketing

- Right Place, Right People Marketing

Client Referrals

Client referrals are the most common marketing technique used by all financial advisors. According to a study by Cerulli Associates, nearly 50 percent of new clients come from client referrals, so advisors who effectively facilitate client referrals can grow their business by 7 percent to 8 percent a year. And according to Russ Alan Prince's study of millionaires in his book, *Cultivating the Middle-Class Millionaire*, of the "loyal" (most satisfied) millionaire clients, 70 percent indicated that they were likely to refer investors to their primary advisor in the next 12 months. Yet only 10.7 percent of advisors actually asked clients for referrals.

My own experience validates both the Cerulli and Prince studies. When I would review client surveys, they always showed that satisfied clients were willing to provide referrals to their advisors. Yet I consistently see that many advisors never execute the client referral marketing technique because they don't have proactive referral processes in their practice whereby clients are consistently asked for referrals. A proactive referral process should include asking each significant client relationship for referrals in a professional way at least once a year.

Many of our top advisors incorporate the "client referral" marketing technique into their practices every day. For example, John evolved his marketing techniques from cold-calling to focusing on generating referrals when he realized that often his competitors didn't show interest in their prospects' lives beyond business. He realized that his focus on building relationships with clients and prospects led to many client referrals. He states, "I [would meet] a prospect, [someone] 50 years old, and at the time I was 26. The prospect thinks, 'He's a nice, sharp-looking kid. He listened to me for an hour and I like him.' When I built that kind of rapport, I'd ask him if he could think of three successful people that I should see, and I usually got some referrals."

Joseph built a referral network from the physicians he targeted. His strategy was to meet with one of the doctors he was working with every month in the physician's lounge at the local hospital. It turned into a great way for a client to introduce him to the other doctors in his practice. Joseph saw that his clients became his advocates and would introduce him to other doctors. Today, Joseph averages about $25 million in new assets each year from client referrals. He estimates he gets 20 to 25 referrals a year from clients, and a number of those referrals end up as clients. He tries to ask for a referral once a year from his 200 client relationships, and he gets a new client about 10 percent to 20 percent of the time that he asks.

Since early in his career, John knew that the key to business growth was getting his clients to identify other people who had money, and then getting them to introduce these people to him. "You have to be willing to ask," John says, "and I will ask all the time because I believe I offer something special and will do a great job for anyone referred to us." John believes you can't ask your clients enough for referrals, and part of that strategy is letting your clients know you are ready to take on new clients. John asks his clients for referrals by saying, "I have always enjoyed working with you and your wife, and if you know anyone else like yourselves that I could help professionally I would appreciate you thinking of me. I am always looking for new clients like you. Does anyone come to mind right now?"

Anne has been aggressive about asking for referrals from the beginning of her career, too. "I ask for referrals from every client I have. I am very specific, giving them a targeted list of people," she says. "I ask them if they know anyone on the list, and if they do, I ask if they can call them for me and encourage them to accept my call." She would create her list by asking her clients who she should know in their industry.

Greg wants to know as much about his clients as possible, including what charities they donate money to, what boards they sit on, and who they know that he should be talking to. He actively asks for referrals if he feels the client is a "referral type" person. Greg is very direct in his referral approach with clients and believes the right client will be happy to help—in fact, they enjoy it. For example, when Greg finds out that a client is on the board of a company and he is going to be in the area, he will identify another prospect that is also on the same board and ask his client if he can use his name as an introduction, or he'll ask the client to call the prospect and let the person know that he will be calling.

Rob shared that 70 percent of his best clients have come from referrals. The majority of them have come from the referring source being aware of Rob's expertise in solving a specific problem. Rob's clients are happy to refer customers because he works hard to ensure his clients are "raving fans."

William estimates that four of his top-10 clients have come from referrals. He believes that you have to have a referral mindset when you speak with your existing clients. For him, that means that when people thank him for a good job, instead of saying "You're welcome," he responds, "I appreciate your kind words, but you should realize that if I don't do quality work for you, you're not going to tell your friends and coworkers about me, and that's how my business grows." William will identify a coworker or a neighbor of one of his affluent clients and use the following referral tactic:

> "I noticed that your neighbor/coworker is on my marketing list. I am going to contact him about his financial planning needs and I was wondering if I could share with him that we work together, as long as I don't disclose anything confidential about our relationship."

IMPLEMENTING THE CLIENT REFERRAL PROCESS

The most important step in developing a client referral strategy is to organize yourself to be able to offer every significant relationship the opportunity to refer someone they care about to you at least once a year. Notice I use the word "offer," not "ask." If you are not confident and proud of how you can help clients reach their financial goals, then you will never have a successful practice. If you are proud of your work, you should feel comfortable *offering* your clients the opportunity to help anyone they care about by introducing them to you. This tactic ties directly into the top-advisor mindset of confidence. When I was interviewing the top advisors for this book, after speaking with each one I felt compelled to transfer all my money to them because they were so confident about their ability to manage investments. You need to exude this level of confidence in order to develop an effective referral approach.

Too often advisors assume that asking for a referral links them to the sales profession. If you engage in a true wealth-management practice, you are in a position to help people financially and should be proud to do so. Entire books have been written about the tactics for asking for referrals. I believe the actual tactics are much less important than having the right top advisor mindset. In other words, what you say is actually less important than your confidence and your willingness to follow the process of doing it with every client every year.

I think that it is appropriate to ask your clients for referrals at least once a year: It's frequent enough, but in no way too often. If a client stays with an advisor throughout the year it is a good indication the client is satisfied and, in most cases, will be happy to help.

After having spent more than 25 years as a financial advisor and manager to other financial advisors, and having participated in countless referral training sessions and observing some of the best in the business, I have developed the following eight-step referral process:

Step 1. Ask for a referral at the end of a quarterly or annual planning session (talking face-to-face, for best results). The reason is that a great deal of goodwill is created by investing time with a client, reviewing the plan developed, putting performance in the right perspective, and connecting personally. This is true even in "bear markets," as clients appreciate the investment of your time with them. This quarterly or annual session sets the right stage for the "offer to help."

Step 2. Develop an agenda for the review, and at the bottom of the agenda, include the referral offer. It can be described as "value proposition" or "offer to help" or simply "referrals." If it is included on the agenda, you can't skip it. This method forces you to approach the subject with every significant client.

Step 3. Offer, don't ask. You are a financial professional, not a salesperson, and when you do good work you must let your pride show. Be a financial missionary.

Step 4. Be specific about who you can help. Clients have a much higher probability of thinking of someone if categories of people are provided. Then they can think in specifics, not generalities, when recalling names. Inquire about people going through a change of circumstance in life (e.g., divorce, promotion, relocation, retirement, inheritance, death of a spouse).

Step 5. Ask the client to call the person in advance to let the person know you will be calling in the next week. You can suggest saying something along these lines: "I feel my advisor has done a good job for me and I suggested he contact you. He would like to introduce himself and share his approach, which I have benefited from." Call the referral the next week, as you told the client you would, whether or not the client has contacted the person. It's reasonable to reference the conversation in which the client recommended that you call the prospect.

Step 6. If your client gives you one referral, keep asking if anyone else comes to mind. You will be surprised at how many names a single client can provide.

Step 7. If the client can't think of anyone, set up future client events as another opportunity for the client to provide you referrals.

Step 8 (optional). Do some research in advance and, if necessary, suggest a name of an affluent individual that your client has a high likelihood of knowing.

The following is an example of an annual "offer to help" client referral script:

> "Ms. C, I hope you feel as good about our investment process and relationship as I do. I know that there are many investors who—if they knew about our approach and how we worked with our clients—would like us to help them. Our challenge is that we don't know who those people are. Is there anyone that you know that could benefit from working with us? Specifically, we work best with investors that have investable assets of [state your minimum] and are going through a change of circumstance in their life—as in someone who has recently retired, been promoted, relocated, sold a business, gone through a divorce, or lost a spouse. . . . Does anyone in those circumstances come to mind?"

[Client says: Yes, I can think of one person.]

> "Thank you, could you let them know in advance that I will contact them next week to introduce myself and share that we work together, would that be okay? Does anyone else come to mind?"

[Client: No, I can't think of anyone.]

> "Thank you for giving it some thought. I wanted to let you know that I will be hosting some client events this coming year for my best clients, like yourself. I have two purposes—one as client appreciation, and the other to provide my clients with the opportunity to invite someone who would enjoy the event, and whom I should meet and could potentially help."

Professional Referral Network

A referral from other trusted professionals (not financial advisors) is the number-one way that millionaires find their financial advisors. This is according to market research done by Russ Alan Prince in *Cultivating the Middle-Class Millionaire*, and Thomas Stanley in *The Millionaire Next Door*. However, when Prince surveyed financial advisors, he found that professional referrals only accounted for 30 percent of their new clients while client referrals accounted for the majority. There seems to be a disconnect between how millionaires choose their advisors and how advisors acquire their millionaire clients. It shows that most advisors don't fully recognize the marketing opportunity of developing a professional referral network. Chapter 7 will go in detail on the implementation steps for developing a professional referral network.

Niche Marketing and Warm Calling

Niche marketing occurs within a specialization. The question all affluent investors ask is, "Why should I do business with you?" And the advisor should be able to answer, "Because I specialize in working with individuals like you." All wealthy investors believe they have unique financial needs and they would much rather work with someone who is a specialist, rather than a generalist who works with everybody and anybody.

If a financial advisor targets a new prospect and that person is remotely or tangentially connected with them through their specialization and/or advanced research, it should not be considered a cold call. Rather, this marketing is referred to as a *warm call*. Warm calling differs from cold calling because while you are targeting individuals that you currently have no relationship with, you have done research in advance on the prospect, can provide references, and are calling as an "insider" rather than an "outsider." The "warm call" is part of targeted networking within a specialized field. Both Ross and

Anne have mastered warm calling within niche markets and are committed to this strategy.

ROSS WARM-CALLS CEOS

Ross's niche market is "money in motion" as it relates to executives and business owners. One of the reasons he chose to focus on them was that they were relatively easy to find: It's relatively easy to get information on a senior executive of a public company on the internet. His niche marketing process involves warm calls for the initial contact.

Ross's partner does a high-level screen on the executives before they are contacted, finding out as much as they can before the initial call. The team targets executives they believe have at least $1 million in investable assets. They have developed a prospect list of between 500 to 600 qualified executives of public companies and successful private companies, many of whom may be potential IPO opportunities. On pre-IPOs, their best sources to identify companies ready to potentially go public are the EDGAR database, the Securities and Exchange Commission (www.sec.gov), and IPO.com. They look for S-1 filings (initial registrations). They also scan the local papers to identify money-in-motion opportunities.

On average, 10 percent of their prospecting calls result in appointments. If they get an appointment, they usually have a high likelihood of converting the prospect into a client. They have found the best way to reach these executives is to call early in the morning (before 8:00 a.m.) or late in the afternoon (after 5:00 p.m.) to avoid their screeners (aka their secretaries or assistants).

The objective of the first appointment is to gather information, build rapport, identify "hot buttons," and briefly share their expertise. An example of the initial warm-call script is as follows:

"My name is Ross, and I am with XYZ Financial. I will be brief. I specialize in working with corporate executives with local public companies. I know you are the chief operating officer and have been an important part of the company's recent success—congratulations. Specifically, my expertise is in providing successful senior executives like you with liquidity, hedging, concentrated stock, and tax minimization strategies. I am confident I could add value to your current investment situation. Would you be available for a brief introductory appointment?"

Ross provides an example of how his team approached a local company that had just been sold. They located this "money-in-motion" opportunity in the local paper. The first step was to find the owner's e-mail address and send him the following message in order to make an introduction:

"Mr. B, with great interest I read that you sold your business to ABC Inc. I read that you started the business ten years ago with one facility and now you have dozens. That's a fantastic accomplishment. Congratulations. I run a high-net-worth practice for XYZ Financial here in town. Our team has combined experience of _____ years. We specialize in working with successful entrepreneurs like you. I would like to invite you to have coffee or lunch to see how we might work together in the future."

At the end of the e-mail, Ross puts a link to his team's website, so the recipient is able to see his team, expertise, and background. Ross then follows the e-mail with a phone call, using this script:

"Mr. B, this is Ross at XYZ Financial, and I sent you an e-mail the other day. I just wanted to tell you again how impressed I am with your story. I don't know anything about you other than what I read in the paper, but I deal with a lot of successful people; in fact, I most enjoy working with self-made people. Can I buy you a cup of coffee as an opportunity to learn more about you and share the process we use in working with successful individuals like yourself?"

And if the person asks what the purpose is, Ross has a response at the ready:

"The purpose is for you and me to get to know each other. I'd like to find out more about you and share what our capabilities are relative to your situation. I would like the opportunity to earn your business. Let's get something on our schedules. What works for you?"

ANNE WARM-CALLS TO SUCCESSFUL EXECUTIVES

Anne sends an introductory letter in advance of her calls, and she always researches the individual before she contacts them so that she can reference their background on her initial contact. Despite her current success as a top advisor, Anne continues to make warm calls every Friday. She estimates that she makes 25 calls on Fridays and reaches one or two new prospects. She has been told that she is very persistent: To her, "no" means "call me back in six months." Once, a prospect she contacted told her, "Trust me; you don't want me as a client." According to Anne, "I responded by saying, 'Trust me, you need to meet with me, and here's why.' So he met with me, and he is a $35 million client now."

Anne's strategy on a warm call is to suggest that the prospect's current advisor may not have the right level of expertise. The dialogue that works best for her is as follows:

"Mr. /Ms. Executive: This is Anne and I'm a private wealth advisor. I specialize in working with senior executives like you and have an extensive planning and family-office background. I wanted to encourage you to consider working with someone that has the expertise and sophistication level appropriate for you. I would like the opportunity to meet with you to find out more about your situation and share with you my background and why I am qualified to help you."

If Anne receives the objection, "I'm dealing with someone else right now," she quickly responds: "I expected you would be, but if you would allow me, I would like to e-mail you some questions to ask your advisor, and next week I will call you and provide you my answers to the same questions. You can compare the answers and determine if it would make sense for us to meet."

Depending on who she is talking to, she chooses five or six of the following questions for the prospect to ask about their current advisor:

- How would they protect your exposure to a concentrated position?

- How would they describe a collaring strategy as it relates to a concentrated position?

- What is the best tax strategy to employ as it relates to the exercising of stock options?

- How would they use the "prepaid forward strategy" to hedge your stock position?

- What's their Net Unrealized Appreciation strategy as it relates to your company stock in your 401(k) plan?

- What are their next-generation planning (GRAT, family, and CRT trusts) and tax strategies?

- What about the value of alternative investments as it relates to overall investment performance?

- What about the value of 10b5-1 trading plans?

- What is the applicability of irrevocable life insurance trusts (ILITs)?

❑ What about exchange funds as a tax strategy for concentrated positions?

NETWORKING WITHIN A NICHE

This marketing tactic leverages the advisor's expertise by providing exposure to affluent investors within the niche field. The strategy is for advisors to immerse themselves in the area by getting involved in the pertinent organizations, reading applicable publications, and interacting with target prospects. It is essentially becoming an insider.

Rob provides a perfect example of how an advisor networks within a niche market and does so with impressive results. Rob is very actively involved in a nonprofit organization of entrepreneurs. The organization's name is TIE, which stands for The Indus Entrepreneurs. Rob took a leadership and mentor role in the national organization and eventually opened a local chapter in his market. He then became "in" with entrepreneurs who were successfully building and selling companies.

TIE members at larger technology companies, like Bell Labs or Motorola, would attend the monthly meetings where they would be encouraged to start up their own companies. The successful entrepreneur members would mentor and introduce them to venture capitalists or investment bankers and Merger and Acquisition attorneys. Rob provided mentorship to these aspiring entrepreneurs and in the process built relationships with them. He expanded his leadership role further by starting a local chapter of TIE in his city, which took more than 12 months and a great deal of time and effort to launch. Rob had developed close relationships with the senior officers within the TIE organization, including the president, who eventually became a client. He would call other members of the organization from whom he thought he could get potential business and provide references of other members of TIE that were his clients, which was a positive affirmation for his prospects. He was never reluctant to be proactive in terms of seeking business from people in the organization.

Rob had developed an expertise in concentrated stock and hedging strategies, so his strength tied in with exactly what the entrepreneurs needed. As a result of his networking, Rob developed clients on a national scale and took his business from $2 million to $5 million.

IMPLEMENTING NICHE MARKETING

The first step in integrating this technique is to identify the market. Doing a review of the occupations of your clients should give you a good sense of your natural market; usually one occupation will stand out as predominant. The next step is to immerse yourself in that niche by finding out what national and local associations are affiliated with your niche market and joining them. Identifying and subscribing to any periodicals, newsletters, and journals that are part of your niche market is another important step. I also recommend reading available books written about your niche market. Many firms offer resources and specialists in a particular area; you should tap those internal resources and make this part of the continuing education process. Interviewing your best clients is another excellent way to add to your expertise. Your clients will tell you what industry-related material they read and what associations they belong to as well as the centers of influence within their industry. Call and ask these centers of influence for an appointment to interview them so you can learn more about their industry. The following is an example of how you might approach an individual that is a center of influence within your niche market:

> "Mr./Ms. Center of Influence this is Joe Smith at XYZ Financial, one of my best clients Mrs. Jones mentioned to me that you were a leader in your industry. I specialize in working with successful business owners like yourself and am always working to add to my expertise and knowledge of your industry. I was hoping that you would agree to meet with me

and allow me to interview you to gain additional knowledge of your industry, is there a time next week that would be convenient for you to meet?"

There are two further success principle lessons that apply directly to niche marketing: *specialization* (see Chapter 4) and *professional development* (Chapter 3). The process of developing a high level of expertise is an evolving one, but it should never end. The higher you raise your level of expertise, the harder it will be for others to compete with you.

Once niche markets have been identified and the process of developing a level of expertise has started, the next step is to create a list of targeted prospects to contact. There is so much information available on the Internet that this step shouldn't be difficult. For example, if your area is business owners, you can research them by industry and business size. Business journals and industry periodicals provide a wealth of information. I also recommend developing a board of directors among your clients that are in your niche, as mentioned in Chapter 4.

Once a list of qualified names is developed, make sure that you have researched each name on the list (have some information on them in advance of the initial contact). The objective is to never make a cold call—all contacts should be "warm." Develop your level of expertise, come across as an industry insider, have some references you can use, and know something about the prospect before you contact them. This is not a random cold call if you have done your research in advance and are an expert on whom you are calling—there is a world of difference.

The following script is an example of a niche market warm contact:

"Mr. P, my name is Jan Jones, and I am a financial advisor with XYZ Financial. The reason for my call is that I have built my business working with successful business owners like you. I have committed to developing a high level of expertise in identifying and solving financial issues that most business owners face. I know you have been recognized as an industry leader; in fact, one of my business owner clients, Ed Smith, suggested I contact you. I believe we have a lot in common, and I would appreciate having the opportunity to meet with you and find out more about your circumstances, share my industry background with you, and discuss how I might be able to improve the bottom line of your business. I would be happy to meet at a convenient place and time for you. What would work for you?"

Event Marketing

The event marketing technique lets you take proactive steps to reward your loyal clients or your professional referral network, and at the same time uncover new prospects.

Not all of our top advisors used client event marketing, but the majority do, and the ones that do find it to be very effective. The key behind this marketing technique is helping clients help their advisors. As indicated by the Russ Alan Prince survey of millionaires, most "loyal" clients are willing to provide their advisor with a referral, but they don't always know who to refer. The event marketing technique provides a venue in which loyal clients can easily introduce potential clients to their advisor.

As described in Chapter 5, John likes smaller venues for event marketing and hosts nice dinners at his home for a combination of clients, friends, and prospects. But John also invites all of his significant clients to an annual client appreciation event. The event is held at his country club, with a buffet dinner and open bar and a high-profile speaker as the entertainment. All clients are encouraged to invite a guest that they think John should meet. The prospect can then see firsthand how well John treats his clients and have the opportunity to meet him in a nonthreatening, interesting, and personal way.

William often hosts "market update events" where he recommends investment strategies for the current market environment. He spends some time educating clients on current market conditions and the themes he believes make the most sense. William uses these market updates as a chance to thank his clients for their business, and he allows them to bring along their friends. He sends his clients invitations that say: "We have specifically reserved ten seats for client referrals. Please let us know if you have a friend, coworker, or neighbor who could benefit from our services, and we'll make every effort to accommodate them." In those two sentences, William has made it clear that he is looking for referrals, and he has given his clients an idea of whom to invite. At the event, he greets the prospects in the following way: "It's nice to meet you; we're glad you came with your cousin [the client]. If we could get your name and contact information we've got a follow-up packet we would love to send you." William always follows up on the packet he sent with an invitation for an initial, complimentary introductory or discovery meeting.

William hosts these client events once a quarter and, typically, between 30 and 100 people attend. Once he rented the local zoo and hosted 150 clients and prospects. According to William, "We had one of our team at the front of the zoo, directing people to the tram that took them to the African Pavilion, and as they got off the tram, we took their picture. They were free to roam the African exhibits. After dinner, we did our investment update speech and had tiki torches around the podium. The tables were set with zebra-skin fabric and stuffed animals became centerpieces on the tables. A CD of African tribal music played during the evening; we even draped the pavilion in mosquito netting. We gave our presentation and everybody had a great time. A week later we sent a card to all the clients and prospects that attended with the picture that was taken."

Ross keeps his events small and simple. "If I can take a guy fishing and have a good day, he's mine forever," he says. "I have created a differentiation from the beginning. I'll take pictures of the day and send it to the client and prospects afterward, so that they can remember what a good time they had."

IMPLEMENTING MARKETING EVENTS

While industry surveys clearly indicate that a very high percentage (70 percent) of loyal affluent clients are willing to give referrals to their primary advisor, the willingness to give and the actual act of providing the referral are often different. Your clients may agree to provide a referral, but when the time comes they will tell you that "no one comes to mind right now." Therein lies the challenge, and that's where the event marketing technique is designed to help clients help you. If you provide a nonthreatening venue for clients to provide introductions, they will more likely invite someone for you to meet. Here is my five-step method for organizing client events:

Step 1. Determine the venue and frequency of the client events. Monthly is ideal, if possible, especially if you are just starting out. Plan your event around educational opportunities and outside interests. Educational events (Investment Strategy Sessions) are meant to feature market updates, where you provide your best thinking about the current financial environment and what type of investments you believe work best (e.g., fixed income or equities, and if equities, which types—large cap, small cap, value growth, or international) At the same time, you can review your wealth-management process.

Outside interest events are determined by your clients' interests: Golf or fishing outings, museum tours, performing arts showings, wine tastings, cooking classes, and sporting events are all good examples. Event marketing is more effective if the events are smaller, although an occasional big event can also work well.

Step 2. Invite your clients with the strong encouragement to bring a guest. It is appropriate to suggest someone that you would like to meet that your client knows. Assure your clients that the focus of the event is about making an introduction, and nothing else. Your clients will feel more comfortable once they understand that you are not pressuring their guests for business. Invite your professional referral sources by themselves or with one of their clients, someone they would like to introduce to you. Include invitations to the prospects in your pipeline.

Step 3. During the event itself, make sure that you interact and begin the relationship development process with your clients' guests and existing prospects. This is not about soliciting business; it's about the relationship-building process. If appropriate, invite them to either another fun event or start the transition process from personal to business relationship by inviting them to your next educational strategy sessions.

Step 4. Begin the follow-up process at the end of the investment strategy session by suggesting that you would appreciate your guests accepting a follow-up contact from you to learn more about your wealth-management process.

Step 5. The follow-up contact should be done as soon as possible after the event and should include a thank-you for attending. It can also include another invitation to your next educational market update or an invitation to a complimentary discovery meeting (where you can learn more about their circumstances and share your wealth-management process in more detail, to see if there might be a potential fit in working together).

Right Place, Right People Marketing

Our top advisors make sure that they put themselves in the position to meet affluent individuals, build relationships, and over time, transition many of these relationships into business. It is the most powerful marketing technique of all, but it can also be the most challenging because of its long-term orientation. Throughout this book I share some of the ways that our top advisors put themselves in the "right place." In particular, Chapter 8 highlights the success principle of nonprofit involvement as a key strategy in the implementation of this marketing technique.

It's not hard to meet the right people at the right place, but the "art" comes in transitioning your relationship with affluent people from a personal contact to a business appointment. I have been asked by advisors over the years how to "market socially." Basically, they are looking for a good line to use during a social occasion to move from fun to business. My answer is that unless a relationship is already built, typically "social marketing" doesn't work. If you do use this marketing technique, then you must understand that it works in three stages. You have to meet the right people at the right place, develop the relationship, and then transition from a personal to business relationship.

Sam implements the "right place, right people" technique as well as any of our top advisors. Sam describes the process as follows: "You have to be around people with money; you can't spend your time talking to people you work with or people that you were buddies with in college that aren't making a lot of money. You've got to commit to and immerse yourself in being around people with money," he says, adding, "I don't have time to spend with people that aren't clients or potential clients. When I got started in the business, I knew as soon as I could afford it, I needed to live in the right place and join the right clubs. I spent the first five years cold-calling, building up a successful business, so I could afford to be in a position to meet rich people. Rich guys in my market like to play golf; they like to fly-fish, so I had to become good at those things. I aligned my activities outside of work with my need to be around people with money. I became a member of a very good country club and immersed myself with people that were rich. The key is to be at the right places with the right people and be someone that those people want to be around."

David believes there is always a moment within every personal relationship where the subject of the markets and investments is going to come up. In his experience, wealthy individuals have lots of problems, and they go to the people they are closest to and respect for solutions. Typical questions he has come across include:

- I just had a liquidity event (i.e., I sold my business). What do you think I should do?

- I'm thinking about selling my business. How should I proceed?

- My mother passed and I have to settle her estate. What are your thoughts?

- What do you think about the municipal bond markets? Yields are low. I'm looking for alternatives. Do you have any thoughts?

- What are you telling your clients about the markets these days? What types of investments do you like right now?

David also believes that if those opportunities don't present themselves and you've developed a good relationship with someone, it is still reasonable to suggest a meeting to discuss business. He doesn't believe you put the personal relationship in jeopardy because the person knows what business you are in. In David's words, "People want to do business with people they know, and most people want to do business with someone they have a relationship with."

William also feels that after a period of time it is perfectly appropriate to suggest a business meeting. He explains, "If you can get to the point where you've had substantial time with these people—and they know you and like you, and they see your work ethic and that what's important to you is important to them—then you can make the following statement: 'We've worked together or known each other for some time, but we have never talked about what I do professionally, and I was wondering, if I dropped by your office, could you give me 30 minutes? I would like to share with you how I could make a positive difference in your investment situation.'"

IMPLEMENTING RIGHT PLACE, RIGHT PEOPLE MARKETING

Drawing from the interviews of our top advisors and my many years of experience, I have developed a tactical four-step process that will enable you to effectively execute this powerful marketing technique. This process will make this marketing technique more "science than art."

Step 1: Right Place. You must put yourself in position for exposure to your target market. This step involves a combination of different actions: Living in the right neighborhood, sending your children to the right schools, belonging to the right clubs, being involved in the community and service organizations, it all contributes to meeting the right people. This advice may seem Machiavellian, but if you want to employ this marketing technique you must find every opportunity to meet your target prospects as part of your lifestyle. It is also an evolutionary process. Like all the top advisors, you start with what you can afford and continue to move upscale as your business increases. For most top advisors there is an almost unconscious upgrade of lifestyle as they became more successful

Step 2: Personal Relationship Development. Identify which of the people that you meet in the right places that you connect with, and then start the process of building relationships with them. Being proactive about the relationship development process is the key. Don't wait for the relationships to develop by themselves. Do things that you and your prospects like to do together. Invite them to dinner; invite them to sporting events, art shows, movies, museum tours; have them meet your spouse and family—all the activities that bring people closer together. Enjoy the process along the way. Most successful people are fun to be with, particularly when you share common interests. All the top advisors would say this is the most fun part of their jobs, and they enjoy this type of marketing the most.

Step 3: Power of Questions. As you are developing relationships with affluent prospects, recognize the power of listening and asking questions. Discuss their profession. Ask how things are going professionally. Ask about their retirement objectives and plans, their children in college, and their financial views. These are among the natural questions that come up as personal relationships are being built. Share with them your views on the markets and appropriate case studies (keeping names confidential) of how you help people (at the right times and as appropriate). Finding out more about their own situations and sharing your expertise, without selling, is your objective in this step.

Step 4: Transition to Business. To turn your personal relationships into a business appointment, you need to have a "transition line" that you are totally comfortable with and are able to interject into your conversation when your prospect gives you the opportunity. This opportunity will come in the form of a question or a statement that is investment related. Examples of such questions might be:

What do you think of the market these days?

What is it exactly that you do for XYZ Financial?

What does XYZ Financial think of the markets?

You have one objective at this point and that is to get a meeting in which investments can be discussed in a professional way. Having these transition lines prepared in advance and ready to use is the key to a seamless personal-to-business progression.

The following are examples of transition lines that have proved to be successful with our top advisors:

Dana says:

◻ "If you are ever interested in chatting with us and see what we really do, I would be delighted to have a cup of coffee with you."

◻ "Stop by the office and see what we do, how we run the practice, or meet my team."

◻ "I've been doing this for a while, but we are not a fit for everyone. Why don't we have lunch and talk about it."

Joseph says:

◻ "If I can ever help you with your investment situation, please let me know. I would be most honored to. If not, I won't ask again."

David says:

◻ "We have known each other for a while and I can tell that you have investment experience. I would appreciate the opportunity to visit with you on how we work with our clients and how we might potentially help you. Would you be open to a lunch meeting?"

William says:

◻ "You know we've worked together for three or four years on the charitable side. I was wondering if you would take 30 minutes sometime and let me explain what I do professionally and see if there is any reason that we should work together."

Other Top Advisor Transition Lines:

◻ "I am serious about growing my business in the community, so if you are ever considering a change or want to know more about our practice, I would be happy to spend a few minutes sharing with you how we work with our clients."

❑ "I provide my best clients with a periodic e-mail on our best thinking on the markets. Would you like me to send you this e-mail?"

❑ "I have an investment strategy market update event planned for my best clients. I would enjoy having you as my guest to hear firsthand what I am advising my clients right now. It is a fun, informal event, and I would love for you come."

❑ "If you would like to know more about our practice and how we work with our clients, I would be happy to invite you to meet our team and share with you our wealth-management process."

❑ "If you would like a second opinion, I would be happy to share with you how we work with our clients."

The Follow-Up Process

Getting the first business appointment with an affluent prospect is the priority, but having a good follow-up process makes the difference in converting the prospect to a client. For example, Ross believes the more he knows about his prospects, the more effective the follow-up. He and his partner will send research that they believe the prospect might be interested in. He says, "There was a wonderful interview the other day with Warren Buffett and we sent it out to our prospects and got the nicest comments that came back." Their e-mails to prospects might also include a funny political cartoon or something personal that the recipient might be interested in.

Mike describes the process of converting prospects to clients in the following way: "Treat your prospects like you would treat a client. Be proactive, be service oriented, and stay in front of them. Send them topical and market-related pieces. Be available to answer questions; take the initiative to discuss changes in developments in their industry and trust and estate planning issues. What you will find is that you are providing better service and resources than they are getting from their current advisor. When the prospect comes to that conclusion, that is when they are ready to become a client. If you want someone to become a client, treat them like a client."

In Anne's case, her first appointment includes some fact-finding, and she shares her expertise on how she can help the prospect. The second meeting is getting into statements, and by the third meeting she is providing a proposal. She typically has a high closing rate by the third appointment, but for those prospects that don't become clients, she is very persistent. At first she contacts them once a week after she meets with them; if they are not ready to make a decision to make a change right away, she moves them to a monthly follow-up.

◻ ◻ ◻

Our top advisors have all recognized that marketing is the lifeblood of this business. Despite their tenure, they never stop marketing themselves. Your marketing efforts and prospect pipeline are leading indicators of your future success. The "secret of success" in this business is proactively putting yourself in front of increasing numbers of affluent investors, building relationships with them, and transitioning those relationships to doing business. If you are committed to developing a top advisor practice, you must also be committed to proactively marketing.

7

LESSON SEVEN
Professional Referral Networks

BUILDING RELATIONSHIPS with wealthy investors is the key to success. But a second type of relationship our top advisors all encourage is one with their professional "influencers." These are the men and women who should be considered referral sources for new prospects. Influencers include CPAs and estate planning attorneys. The professional referral network principle requires commitment, time, preparation, and patience, but I highly recommend it for anyone who aspires to grow their practice and become a top advisor.

In his book *The Millionaire Mind*, Thomas Stanley indicates that the primary way millionaires find financial advisors is through other

114 I THE MILLION-DOLLAR FINANCIAL ADVISOR

advisors, specifically their CPA and their attorney. In *Cultivating the Middle-Class Millionaire*, Russ Alan Prince makes the same finding: The more affluent the investors are, the more likely they will find their financial advisor through their CPA or attorney.

The reason affluent investors rely so heavily on their other professional advisors for referrals is simple: trust. They already know their CPA or their attorney, so it is logical that they would trust their judgment in recommending a financial advisor. The referral method takes a lot of the risk out of a high-consequence decision.

The referral source stands to gain from creating a high-quality relationship as well. Their value to their client and their influence increases if they can recommend a financial advisor who really does a good job. However, there is also great risk to them if the financial advisor does not do a good job for their clients. Because of these high stakes, the influencer is going to proceed with caution, making sure to have a high degree of confidence in the financial advisor being recommended.

This dynamic is what the professional referral source lesson is all about: You must build a strong professional and personal relationship with influencers before a referral will be made. Financial advisors must establish themselves as a value-added resource, primarily by educating the influencer on the financial markets as it relates to their professional value to clients. It is exactly the same concept as described in the relationship success principle in Chapter 5. A relationship of trust must be built, and that takes time. By establishing yourself as an educator, adding value to the influencer's practice, and all the while building a personal relationship, you are setting the stage for the professional referral source to recommend their clients to you.

Best of all, if a professional referral source refers a client to you, chances are very high that the person will actually become a new client for you. Typically, an influencer will only refer clients when there is a problem or need for an advisor. That's why a professional referral is as close to a "lay-up" as there is in this business.

Charles—A Master of Influencer Marketing

One of the top advisors with whom I worked, Charles, was extraordinary in his approach to professional influencers. He built an extremely successful financial practice through his referral sources. By his tenth year, Charles was doing more than $3 million in business with $500 million in client assets. Through his referral sources he was bringing in, on average, more than $50 million in new assets annually. Charles had a refined process of developing referral sources that was the best I had ever seen, even better, frankly, than the methods used by other top advisors I had interviewed.

Charles started in this business without a single contact. He had no special circumstances: He was 26 years old with no past experience in the financial world. In the beginning, Charles recognized that if he was going to be successful in building a professional referral source network, he was going to have to be very knowledgeable about the financial markets. He wanted to be a true resource to the professionals he was going to build relationships with. Charles understood that if he added value to the businesses of his network of influencers, they would have confidence in his ability to help their clients, and they would in turn provide referrals. Charles's challenge was that he had no financial background, and he soon realized he knew even less than he thought he did. He discovered that he really had two full-time jobs. One was learning about the financial markets and the other was building his practice. It was during this ramp-up stage that Charles discovered that to be successful at this business, he had to be committed to working harder than he ever had in his life.

Charles became a true student of the markets. He read everything he could about them, including textbooks, business periodicals, his firm's research, and anything he could get his hands on that he thought could accelerate his learning curve. Charles made 600 flash-cards with a financial term on the front and the definition of the term on the back and studied them constantly. He started to put together a large body of knowledge, connecting the dots, raising his confidence, and putting together wonderful presentations.

However, while his financial knowledge was growing, the development of his business was not going as well. After a lot of soul-searching and self-evaluation, Charles knew that he was putting too much emphasis on becoming a "professor of finance" and was missing the relationship side of the formula. He was so busy pre-senting and sharing his financial knowledge that he wasn't finding the opportunity to bond and build rapport with his professional referral network and other prospects. Charles had the ability to empathize, and he really did care about people, but he had sup-pressed this ability because of his focus on acquiring and sharing his newfound knowledge.

Charles changed his approach and began to combine his knowledge of finance with a new focus on the relationship, and his business success began to improve. One day, he had an appointment with some prospects who had just sold a business and had "millions" to invest as a result. But Charles really didn't care; he was tired and emotionally drained after a long day of pre-senting, selling, and being "on." So Charles took a different approach with this couple: He passively explained the markets, the importance of asset allocation, and planning. He wasn't try-ing to sell; he was simply educating these people. He was taking the complex, unknown, and intimidating financial markets and he was explaining them in the simplest terms. Surprisingly, the prospects were very impressed and decided to do business with him immediately. Charles had finally transcended from financial professor to salesman to teacher. In his mind, he had finally "bro-ken the code." If he applied his hard work, financial knowledge, empathy, and teaching emphasis and took this powerful combination of skills to his professional referral network, he knew he would be met with great success.

This epiphany led Charles to develop a formal presentation that explained how capital markets worked, and his investment process. He was able to present this material in a way that was easy to understand for his clients, prospects, and referral sources. In terms of developing relationships with potential professional referral sources, he started by thinking about what professional advisors would most be interested in knowing about the financial markets, and how he could provide that knowledge. He worked with professionals the same way he did with his prospects and clients: by educating them on the basics, making this complex industry more understandable. He quickly learned that these professionals believed that they should know more about the financial markets, and it created anxiety for them that they didn't. According to Charles, "My professional referral sources feel a sense of responsibility for something that is not in their core competency." The reaction of his professional referral sources was the same as his clients and prospects: They appreciated his approach.

Next, Charles developed a "white paper" library that contained current, relevant financial and investment information that he knew his referral sources would be interested in. He collected data on what he believed would add value and be interesting to the influencers in his network including the following topics:

- Management of bonds in the context of the alternative minimum tax

- The best investments for charitable remainder trusts (CRTs)

- The importance of the Monte Carlo simulation in determining cash flow for retirees: the calculation of the probability of investment returns based on the way assets in a portfolio are allocated

▢ The value of geometric vs. arithmetic returns

▢ How to invest money for estate planning

▢ Alternative investments and their tax implications

▢ Modern portfolio theory

▢ The importance of asset allocation and the tools available to design portfolios

▢ The importance of financial planning and the types of plans available

▢ Understanding the current investment climate

▢ How to best position clients if they have a liquidity event

▢ Innovative credit/lending opportunities

▢ Municipals, corporate, and treasury bonds and when to best utilize them

▢ How to help recently divorced women manage their spending through Monte Carlo analysis

▢ Case studies of how he helped clients and how that might apply to the influencer's client

Charles's mission was to bring the investment world to his professional referral network of influencers and share how that was relevant to them and their clients. Charles changed his role from financial encyclopedia to salesman to "teacher." It turned out that the educational opportunities were limitless, and continually changing, so there would be an endless supply of information his referral sources needed. In Charles's words, "At any given time I could come up with at least six new relevant educational concepts that I could share with my network." Case studies were especially effective because they would give the professional referral sources an idea of how Charles could help their clients.

Getting the Appointment

When he first got started in the business Charles's first goal was to get a face-to-face appointment with an influencer. Charles would go to office buildings and collect business cards of CPAs and attorneys. He would call these professionals and say: "My name is Charles, and I work for XYZ Financial. I would like to have the opportunity to meet you, learn about your practice, and potentially establish a professional relationship." The statement was honest, direct, and straightforward. At least 50 percent of the time he would get an appointment. He set an objective of scheduling four appointments a day: breakfast, mid-morning, lunch, and dinner.

For the first appointment he had two goals: to create a friend and future advocate, and to set himself up as a valuable resource for his referral source. He spent the majority of the meeting finding out about the influencer's practice, answering questions, and positioning himself. Sometime during the first meeting Charles would also schedule a second meeting, so that he could share his investment approach.

Charles found that CPAs and estate attorneys felt that all financial advisors were the same, and his objective for the second meeting was to differentiate himself in a positive way. He would provide a brief presentation on his investment process and set up the education and relationship-building process. He ended the second appointment by saying the following:

> "You must get a lot of people like me coming around all the time, wanting your clients, and that's not my intention. I have tremendous resources I can offer you, and I want to become one of the arrows in your quiver. Through the process I want to build a long-lasting relationship with you, based upon mutual professional respect. And, if I can convince you down the road, through the process of really educating you on what it is that I do, I would be glad to accept a referral from you. It turns out I'm going to be back here three weeks from now, and

I would like to share with you some alternative minimum tax strategies that I think you would find helpful to your practice. Can we schedule a short meeting when I'm back in the area?"

At least once a month Charles would visit each of his influencers with the intent of building a closer personal bond, providing education, and increasing their confidence in him. Charles invited them to sporting events, lunches and dinners, and quarterly educational forums. At the forums he would cover a timely and relevant topic that would help his influencers look smarter so they could better advise their clients. Often he would make the presentation, but he would also sometimes invite an "outside expert" to be part of the seminar. Charles never relied on phone calls or e-mail other than for setting up follow-up meetings, which were always done in person.

A Long-Term Approach

There is no shortcut to building a good relationship with a professional referral source. Charles found that it typically took 18 months of relationship building and educating a referral source before he could begin to expect a referral. In many cases it took longer, but once the referral came and the client was satisfied, the rate of referrals accelerated. At times Charles was getting three referrals a month, and sometimes even more.

Through a referral from one influencer, Charles once ended up developing accounts with all the senior executives at a major technology firm. As Charles tells the story, "One of the cards I got when I was walking through buildings in my early years was the card of a family law attorney. I met with her and we developed a good professional relationship. Her husband was the CEO of a small semiconductor company that was bought by a larger, publicly traded technology firm. He became president of one of the divisions and introduced me to the head of marketing for the entire firm. He became a client and introduced me to the rest of the senior executives, and I opened accounts with every one of them."

Another influencer was a CPA who advertised himself as a financial services specialist. However, Charles quickly realized that this CPA's definition of "financial services" was different from his own. Charles knew that he could help this CPA live up to his billing. Because of his approach and how he helped this CPA, he was provided with 35 referrals over the years.

The Reverse Approach

Once Charles built up his client base, he didn't have to cold-call for potential influencers. Instead, he would ask his current clients if he could contact their CPA and/or estate attorney for their benefit. The client always agreed, and the CPA or estate attorney was happy to make the first appointment as a business favor. Charles would approach the CPA or estate attorney in the following way:

> "Jane Smith is a mutual client of ours, and I'm really interested in making sure that we are completely coordinated on everything we do for her. I'd like to come and meet you. And by the way, Jane speaks very highly of you, and I'd like to learn more about your practice because I'm always looking for top professionals to include in my professional network."

The Numbers

Charles made contact with more than 400 different professional influencers, and actually met with 200 of them. About 100 showed some interest in having an ongoing relationship, 50 became part of his network, and 25 provided multiple referrals. The 50 individuals in his core professional network would attend his quarterly educational lunches, and they all developed meaningful relationships with him. In the process of building these relationships and educating his professional referral network, he has opened accounts with virtually all his network members. Charles now has a team member who devotes his entire day to scheduling monthly educational and follow-up meetings with his professional referral source network.

As these relationships developed, Charles would let his CPAs and attorneys know that he would be interested in referrals. Sometimes he took a subtle approach, and other times he was more direct. "The referral source would ask how it was going, and I would respond that we are building our business and currently have the capacity to add clients," Charles says.

He also makes it clear to his referral network that he is not always in a position to reciprocate. His value to his sources of recommendation is to enhance their practice through education and resources, and to reflect well on them by taking good care of the referrals provided.

Three Constituents

Charles believes he has three important constituents in his practice:

- Clients
- Prospects
- Professional referral sources

According to Charles, he has to move forward with these constituents all the time, asking himself every day what he is doing to advance these relationships. He believes that as long as he spends every day focused on his constituents, his business will continue to grow.

Charles's Best Tips for Building a Professional Referral Network

- Ask a CPA or attorney to meet with a mutual client to collaborate on investment and tax strategies.

◻ If a mutual client relationship doesn't exist, invite the CPA or attorney to a meeting to learn more about their practice.

◻ Tell all of your significant clients that you can do your best work on their behalf if you are in contact with their CPA or attorney. Ask for their permission to introduce yourself to their other advisors and offer to collaborate on their behalf.

◻ During the first meeting with a CPA or attorney, discuss the mutual client and learn more about the other professional's practice. Schedule a second meeting.

◻ In the second meeting, provide a concise but professional presentation of your investment process and show how you differentiate yourself.

◻ In the second meeting, offer to be a resource for influencers and agree to educate and share information that helps their practice.

◻ Hand-deliver your "white paper" information (timely and relevant investment information and ideas with regard to the capital markets) to the influencer's practice.

◻ Develop continuing education seminars with influencers regarding relevant tax and investment topics.

◻ Host fun relationship-building events for your influencer network, without clients attending.

Tim—A CPA's Perspective

To complement Charles's perspective on developing a professional referral network, I interviewed a number of CPAs to gain an understanding of how they view the relationship between themselves and financial advisors. Tim is the senior partner of a very successful local accounting services firm.

Charles's process of developing a successful professional network was completely validated by Tim, who said that Charles had devised the best way for a financial advisor to approach a professional influencer. According to Tim, the relationship was the most important factor in providing referrals. "You find people you like, relationships that you have common values with and common business principles," Tim says. In developing a relationship with someone, Tim tries to understand what kind of person they are and what their values are. In Tim's words, "If you sit down with somebody and have a conversation with them, you walk away with an impression. Was the conversation about them or was it about you? An advisor will never get a referral from me if it's all about them. If financial advisors want to make a good impression on me, it's about what they can give, rather than what they can get."

Typically, Tim will refer clients when they come to him with a problem that he cannot solve. His philosophy is if his clients need something and he can help by making a referral, that's part of his job. "I refer my clients to advisors that have an expertise in the particular area that is needed," he says. "For example, if I have an executive working on a succession plan or a merger and acquisition, I will refer her to an advisor that is an expert in that area [and] who I know is going to take care of her."

The most common way Tim develops a referral relationship with financial advisors is by working together with them for the benefit of a mutual client. The advisor may bring Tim into a meeting if he needs to be aware of the client's investment situation as it relates to the client's taxes. Tim recommends that advisors look at their best clients and develop a plan on how they could involve a CPA in a planning meeting that would be tax-related. He says, "Doing business together you can see how each other works. If you're able to sit down and go through a case together, the advisor can impress me without telling me how good they are. Then, the next time a potential referral comes up, you will probably think about them. You are more confident that the financial advisor will be good because you saw how good they were with the client, as well as their professionalism and expertise."

Tim's reservation about financial advisors is clear. "The worst thing about referring a client to a financial advisor is that I've become responsible for [that person's] success. There is an absolute risk in referrals, and that's why I have to be very careful with whom I refer," Tim says. "I've lost clients because I've referred them to financial advisors that have done a poor job, and if I haven't lost them, I've lost their confidence. On the other hand, if I can refer my clients to good advisors and they are taken care of, it enhances my relationship and I know I have that client forever."

The personal relationship also plays an important part in developing a referral relationship. According to Tim, "I don't do business with anybody that I wouldn't play golf with or go to a concert or ball game with. The best approach is to build a good relationship."

Again, E-Mail Isn't the Way to Build Relationships

Tim agrees with our top advisors, too, about the ineffectiveness of e-mails in terms of building relationships. "I'm not interested in working with a salesman. I get three or four e-mails a week of investor updates by different investment firms. The information they include is very easy to attain, but frankly I'm too busy to read most of it," the CPA says.

Instead, Tim suggests creating a referral network through personal meetings, targeting CPAs with common interests, including growing their own practices. He suggests focusing on individuals looking to network themselves. Don't waste time with people who are unwilling or unable to provide referrals. "If you can identify those things early, you won't waste your time," he says.

Tim gives at least 50 percent more referrals than he gets, and he's okay with that. In Tim's words, "The referral network with financial advisors is not reciprocal. CPAs get most of their referrals and business from bankers, and so it's not a circular relationship."

Tim's Numbers:

❑ Number of financial advisors he refers clients to each year: 8

❑ Average number of referrals per advisor: 3 (24 total in a year)

❑ Number of calls a year from different advisors wanting to meet with him: approximately 30

❑ Number of additional financial advisors he might refer business to in the future: 3

❑ Average time for Tim to make a referral from first meeting a financial advisor: 18 months

Implementing Lesson #7

As you can see, the numbers are too compelling for any motivated advisor to ignore. The first step, then, is to recognize the importance of this success principle and make a commitment to develop a professional source network.

Before implementing the influencer referral source network strategy, it is important to have the right mindset. You must be patient and know in advance that developing relationships with CPAs and estate attorneys takes a long time. According to both Charles (a financial advisor) and Tim (a CPA), it takes on average 18 months from the first contact to the time an actual referral is provided. Additionally, for every ten CPA and attorney appointments a financial advisor gets, only one will become a referral source. However, don't be discouraged: There are lots of CPAs and attorneys out there. For example, in Charles's market in a major metropolitan area, there are 4,500 CPAs and attorneys.

Be prepared to build a relationship with the professional influencer by educating, not selling or presenting. The objective is to build a trusting relationship by providing relevant information that helps the referring professional's practice. The same principles learned in Chapter 5, on building a relationship focus, apply here.

Your goal should be to develop at least three professional referral sources that provide ongoing referrals. Using Tim's numbers, let's assume that getting three client referrals a year is a reasonable expectation once a professional relationship is established. If an advisor has three referral sources and gets a total of nine referrals from them, and then closes 90 percent of the referrals provided, the advisor should generate eight new relationships a year.

Three Steps to a Successful Influencer Meeting

Step 1: Target your influencers. The first way to meet new influencers is to work with your existing significant clients. Ask them if they are satisfied with their CPA and estate planning attorney and if you could contact these professionals for a meeting. If you don't have a client base that can be leveraged, use the direct and straightforward approach, as Charles used when he first got started, by simply asking other professionals for an opportunity to meet with you. I recommend the following script as a way to introduce yourself:

> "My name is Jan Jones, and I am a financial advisor with XYZ Financial. I am in the process of getting to know the best CPAs in our market with whom to develop a professional relationship. As I continue to build my practice, it is among my highest priorities to build a network with the right professionals. I also believe there is a high likelihood that in the future we will share mutual clients. I would like the opportunity to meet with you and find out more about

your practice. When would be a convenient time for us to get together for an introductory meeting?"

Step 2: Create a pitch book. Next, put together a pitch book (a formal presentation) that describes your firm, your team, and your wealth-management process. The pitch book should clearly show CPAs/attorneys what you do and how you do it. Include the following elements in your presentation:

- Team description

- Your background and experience

- Your firm's description

- Your specialty

- Resources available (e.g., Monte Carlo analysis, asset allocation tools, financial plans, retirement analysis)

- Investment process and philosophy (wealth-management process)

Step 3: Develop a "white paper library." This group of documents will serve as the foundation for the educational process you as a financial advisor will provide on a monthly basis to your professional referral network. Charles's list of topics is a perfect outline for the development of the "white paper" library. A very effective educational topic is to share case studies from your own clientele.

Outline of Prospecting Meetings

The first meeting should be about gathering information that is focused on the influencer and this professional's business. Examples of potential questions could include:

- Tell me about your practice.

- Tell me about your background.

- What kind of clients are you looking for? Describe your ideal client.

- What is your specialization?

- How do you get new clients?

- Are you interested in continuing education offerings?

- What resources would be valuable to your practice that could be provided by an investment firm or professional?

- Can you share with me the type of relationship you have with other investment professionals?

- How can someone like me best help you and your practice?

At the end of the first meeting, you should make a short statement about your financial advisor practice and the value you can provide. You should also schedule a second appointment to share information about your practice and specifically how it could be used as a resource. (Refer to the "Getting the Appointment" section of this chapter, to review once again how Charles, our master of influencer marketing, positions himself during these meetings.)

The second meeting should have two objectives. You will present your pitch book and set the foundation for the ongoing educational process. This is the time to share how you can provide timely, relevant information and resources that will help the other professional advisor's existing practice.

Now the stage should be set for scheduling monthly follow-up meetings (no longer than 30 minutes) where you can stop by and provide educational materials. The white paper library provides the basis for these ongoing meetings. The continuing appointment process is simply a way to provide resources and education that is customized to the needs of the influencer. Some of these monthly meetings can be more social in nature. For example, Charles arranges a special luncheon quarterly for the 50 members of his professional network. The objective is to educate, build, and maintain a long-term relationship of value and trust with these professionals.

Other Types of Influencers

CPAs and estate attorneys are not the only individuals considered influencers. Other resources you can tap include business brokers, investment bankers, mergers and acquisitions attorneys, divorce attorneys, and bookkeepers (non-CPA accountants). The same principles apply: Your primary objective is to enhance their practices through value-added education and resources so that you can build a solid, long-term relationship that ultimately will lead to client referrals.

8

Nonprofit Organization Involvement

A NOT-FOR-PROFIT organization provides value and resources for the benefit of the community, including the performing arts and health, civic, and humanitarian services. The purpose of a nonprofit organization is not to make a profit, but to raise money or provide services for a particular organization. Volunteering with any of these types of groups is not only a good way to give back to the community, but it can be a fully developed marketing strategy for your business. Our top advisors recognize that the most affluent individuals in their communities are very involved in the not-for-profit world. In many instances, these affluent individuals are retired and can direct their energies and talents toward the causes they passionately believe in. As I've said before, very affluent prospects are heavily screened. Typically, they already have an advisor and are heavily prospected. Nonprofit organizations allow access to these individuals; they let you build personal and then business relationships with wealthy people in an organic fashion. However, it must be done the right way. It takes patience and discipline to successfully execute this market strategy and get a return on your time investment. By working with potential prospects in this type of setting, you will have the unique opportunity to showcase and demonstrate your expertise, leadership, and personality.

As you become more involved with nonprofits you have to "pay to play." The most prestigious nonprofits require that you make significant contributions before you can be considered for a position on the board. Yet I believe that this is among the best investment a motivated advisor can make, because of the access you'll gain and the opportunity to develop relationships with the most affluent members of the community. Many of our top advisors individually donate more than $10,000 to nonprofit organizations that they are involved in. They view these expenditures as retained earnings.

Our top advisors typically commit at least five hours a week for their work on behalf of the organizations to which they belong. Often, their spouses are involved in the same organization as well. Or spouses choose other organizations about which they are passionate. In this case, a spouse can leverage the advisor's efforts by providing introductions to a separate group of affluent investors. Many of the top advisors met some of their most affluent clients through the work of their spouse.

Selecting Your Organization of Choice Wisely

One of our top advisors gave his son some advice when he was just starting in the business. His son spent time at the shooting range with younger people who didn't have much money. He advised his son to spend that same time involved in organizations that had successful individuals as members. He pointed toward the local Rotary Club, alumni groups, and religious organizations, all of which are great suggestions for nonprofit involvement.

Because of the work and time required, I suggest that you choose your nonprofit organizations carefully. The work is too hard, time commitment too great, and cost too high not to be interested and believe in the organization's cause. In the end, it is the similar passion that you and affluent individuals share that forms the bond that translates to a business relationship.

Most of our top advisors started their involvement in nonprofit organizations on a small scale. They chose organizations that they could afford to join, including local religious groups, local chambers of commerce, community service organizations like Kiwanis, Jaycees, and Rotary clubs, outside interests like Ducks Unlimited, and college alumni groups. Typically these organizations gave them access to prospects and required very little financial commitment.

By starting early in their careers with the nonprofit marketing strategy, our top advisors developed the leadership and relationship-building skills that they needed when the stakes were higher. From their involvement in these smaller and more affordable organizations, they also built the foundation for their business with many prospects who later became clients.

Dana Made Joining Nonprofits Her Marketing Strategy—A Case Study for Successful Implementation

One of our most impressive stories involves a top advisor who made a major commitment to the nonprofit world. Dana moved her practice to a very affluent market and realized that many of her target prospects had retired or didn't have to work. She realized that many of these affluent individuals were directing their talents, energy, and resources to nonprofit organizations in her market.

Dana created an organized approach as a marketing strategy to grow her business. Her first step was to identify the major donors and board members in her market. She began by cross-referencing board members and their levels of donations to find out which individuals in her community were most involved and contributed the most to nonprofit organizations. She viewed the websites of the most prestigious and high-visibility organizations in her community and compiled a list of board members by name. Often these websites will also post general levels of donations; otherwise, she contacted the nonprofit and asked for an annual report or a "program" prepared for a recent gala or fund-raising event. The minimum contribution level she looked for was at least in the $5,000 to $10,000 range. This screening process yielded the names of 150 individuals that she wanted to get to know, as well as the names of the boards these people were affiliated with. She was specifically looking to target different types of nonprofit boards that would provide a diversity of ages and interests among her prospects.

Her research showed the top-10 donors on her list belonged to one or more of four different nonprofit boards. She chose three of them based on diversity and her personal interest in them and the opportunity they could provide her in building relationships with many of the other affluent individuals on her target list. The nonprofit boards she joined included the local symphony and another performing arts group. Her husband also joined a high-profile board that had a sports orientation. Dana was able to join the boards by getting the nomination and endorsements of a few influential individuals she had already built relationships with. During the interview process, she indicated her strong interest in the nonprofit's mission and her willingness to make a significant financial contribution. The minimum level of contribution required for these board positions was $10,000. This investment of time and money was worth it for Dana, because her involvement resulted in more than $70 million in new assets last year from the successful implementation of her not-for-profit strategy.

Becoming a Leader

As Dana demonstrated, being a leader in your chosen nonprofit is essential in making this strategy work. It is not enough just to be in the same organizations as your target prospects; you have to make a good impression. The best place to take on a leadership role is to join a committee that plays to your strengths. While board memberships are important, the committees are where the real work gets done. The best ones can showcase your strengths and expertise and might include finance, business development, and nominating committees. The social committee should be avoided because it is difficult to showcase professional expertise there. Female advisors in particular need to avoid the "gala" or social committees because it can cast them in a traditional role that they may want to avoid.

Your objective is to demonstrate your intelligence, your added value, your level of engagement, and your ability to be the "star student." Use the leadership opportunity to showcase financial experience with investments and current clients. For example, if you are working on the finance committee, you can state: "Based on my experience as a financial advisor, in the current investment environment we should consider the following." Or, "I have given my clients the same recommendations that I make to this committee of how we should be investing our assets in the current environment."

In these examples, you are sharing in an appropriate context your expertise in the market and your role as a professional investment advisor. This makes it clear to the other committee members what you do and your level of expertise. There is also a natural psychological effect that occurs when an advisor has done good work for a nonprofit. The committee and board members will naturally transfer their good feelings toward the work that you have done for the nonprofit to the quality of work you are capable of doing professionally as an investment advisor. This is the "halo effect," and it is an important part of the nonprofit marketing strategy.

Raising Money

Another excellent way for you to meet wealthy individuals is to be involved in fund-raising for the organization. First, you can showcase your expertise in philanthropic strategies by referencing strategies you currently use with your clients. Because of the experience most advisors have in asking for money, they are better at approaching affluent supporters of the organization and soliciting donations.

Requesting donations also gives you the opportunity to connect with other target prospects—outside of the board—on a one-to-one basis, rather than in a committee or group setting. Another benefit is that most donations come with an invitation to a "big event" sponsored by the nonprofit. Spending an evening with wealthy prospects and their spouses is as good as it gets for a first meeting.

Many of our top advisors choose to host nonprofit events at their home. This makes a good impression on everyone that attends and puts the advisor in the best possible light. You not only appear as a committed fund-raiser, but also as a "real person" to the other members of the organization. Many of the top advisors that are involved in nonprofits share examples of how they met some of their most significant relationships through their fund-raising activities. For example, Jack has always been very involved with the university he graduated from. He has served on the foundation board for a number of years and, as a result, developed relationships with the other alumni, as well as some of the largest donors to the university, some of whom have become among his most affluent clients.

By assuming the role of helping to raise money for a nonprofit, you can offer your insights on other endowment investment strategies and how to raise assets for the organization. One of the strategies is to educate the board members and fundraising committees on philanthropic strategies, including charitable lead and remainder trusts. You can also bring in a trust specialist who either works for your firm or is someone in your network. Dana regularly shares her philanthropic expertise when she hosts meetings on how to raise money, and she has found it to be a successful way to attract potential prospects.

Managing the Money

Another strategy that many top advisors use is to manage the assets of nonprofit organizations. This strategy does not necessarily apply to the organizations that they belong to. The important part of this strategy is to determine the affluence of the board members, and not necessarily the amount of assets the nonprofit has to be managed. By focusing on the wealth of the board members as opposed to the amount of assets the organization itself has to be invested, the advisor will face little competition for management of these smaller nonprofit assets.

Once you have secured the business, you can make formal quarterly presentations to the board on the performance and strategy of the assets under management. These reviews give you the opportunity to talk about the markets, and you'll impress board members with your knowledge and expertise in investing assets. The strategy goes beyond making a good impression: The advisor is in effect marketing her or his capabilities related to investment strategy, philanthropy, and working with affluent individuals.

Dana made a quarterly review presentation to her board for a $100,000 CD portfolio, but she presented it as if it were $10 million. During the presentation, she included an explanation of what she would do in terms of investment strategy when the endowment had more assets. The board was successful at raising more funds, and within five years it in fact became a $10 million portfolio. On top of this, Dana also secured the investment relationship with a board member for more than $10 million in assets.

Building Personal Relationships with Other Board Members

The next step is to build a personal relationship with your targeted nonprofit affluent prospects. By doing good work and showcasing your talents in working committees, you have already set the stage for developing personal relationships. The fact is, doing good work and developing relationships with affluent individuals go hand in hand.

Dana would indirectly target affluent people on her boards that she personally connected with. "I always think it's about the relationship," she told me. "If you develop a good relationship it's mutual. I like them, they like me. I would identify board members that I wanted to develop business relationships with and start the process of [first] developing a personal relationship with them. I would invite them to dinner with a group of other people, either at my home or out. I begin to get to know them socially. Over time, the relationship usually develops to a point where they feel more comfortable talking to me about business."

Weaving Yourself into the Fabric of the Community

The top advisors that are the most successful with the nonprofit marketing strategy went beyond just being involved in organizations; they emerged over time as part of the fabric of the community they lived and worked in. In all cases, this was an evolution that took years to achieve. However, the business impact was exponential as they developed a reputation as an influential community member. Dana adds, "I also felt that I had to be influential in the community in other ways. It's showing up at their kids' games and other significant events in their lives. It's being invested in them and the community."

The reality is that no matter the actual size of the community, it becomes small when it comes to identifying the real leaders. The ultimate execution of the nonprofit strategy is when the advisor reaches the level of a true leader in the community. The barrier of entry to this elite status is high because of the time required. However, any advisor that makes the commitment can become part of that fabric, and the business that will result is worth every bit of the effort.

Forming Your Own Nonprofit

One of the most successful marketing strategies is to organize and start your own nonprofit organization. This requires a great deal of work in the beginning, but the payoff can be very big. For example, Dana formed a debate team at the private school her children attended. Together with several other parents, Dana was able to raise the money to pay for a full-time debate coach for the school, which added to the quality of the educational experience. The debate team was very successful and received a great deal of local press. As a result, Dana was featured as one of the most influential individuals in her affluent community by a highly regarded magazine and named as one of its "Persons of the Year." Not only did Dana get excellent publicity, but the other affluent parents of students on the debate team saw her in action, professionally, in a most positive way. Dana gained several affluent new clients, which she attributes to her efforts with the debate club, including one $10 million relationship. Plus, she recognizes that the publicity was priceless for her reputation in the community.

Another advisor formed a "Dads' Club" at his children's school. Within three years the Dads' Club had 50 active members, including some of the most prominent members of the community. Through fund-raising and volunteer work, the Dads' Club provided the school with well over $50,000. The advisor that started the club was able to showcase his leadership skills and his commitment to the school, and he generated a tremendous amount of goodwill from the community. At the same time, he was able to develop many personal relationships which led to business relationships with other members of the Dads' Club.

In both examples, the schools involved had been in existence for many years, but it was by implementing a fresh, new idea in these settings that both of these advisors were able to raise funds and goodwill. They were seen as leaders in the community, and as a result they built relationships with many target prospects and were able to open several new million-dollar relationships.

Transitioning from Nonprofit to Business

When it comes to transitioning from nonprofit involvement to a business relationship, the overall message from our top advisors is *patience*. In many instances it took as long as seven or eight years before the personal relationship developed into a significant business relationship. However, in all cases the advisors stated that their patience paid off, because these relationships became some of their largest clients.

Our top advisors found that they formed natural connections with many of the affluent individuals they worked with in the not-for-profit world. They shared many common interests and, as their working relationship developed and they got to know the prospective client, they would find and develop opportunities to invite these prospects to join them in other activities—a hunting, fishing, or skiing trip, for example, or a golf outing, an evening of fine dining, a cooking class, or sharing a performing arts or travel experience. Each activity, done together with the future client, brings the advisor closer to the opportunity for a business relationship.

The next step involves preparation. When the inevitable investment questions come up, you need to be ready with a response, I call these transition lines. As we discussed in Chapter 5, the key is to turn the opportunity to your advantage so that you can successfully transition from the personal to a potential business partnership. Here are two examples:

❑ *What if a board member or target prospect asks your opinion of recent market events?* In this situation, you can respond by saying, "I believe the markets will [provide a short explanation], but I have found it is the process of investing that is more important than the markets at any given time. Over coffee I would enjoy sharing with you how we help our clients through our wealth-management process. Could we set up a time and place?"

□ *A relationship you have developed in a nonprofit organization indicates they might be interested in talking to you about investments, but they are currently working with someone else.* The prospect says, for instance, "I am impressed with you, but all my money is with ABC financial," or " I know you are a smart person, but I am already working with someone." Here, you can respond by saying, "I understand that you are working with someone else; my clients are loyal as well. But if you decided to make a change, I would appreciate being on your short list of people that you would consider. I believe we have a unique and successful investment process and I would enjoy the opportunity to share it with you, in the event your circumstances change or if you know someone who would benefit from the way we work."

It is important to make clear to potential prospects that there is exclusivity to your practice: that your strategies are not for everyone. This approach lets the affluent prospect know that you are selective about whom you work with, just as they are in deciding if they want to work with you. Your attitude of displaying the pride you have for your work needs to be conveyed as confidence to potential prospects. An example might be if you are asked what you do at XYZ financial. You can respond, "I work with a select group of families to achieve their long-term financial goals and objectives through our unique wealth-management process. I would be happy to share how we work with our clients, if you would be interested."

The core of the transition process from personal to business is not a one-time opportunity. The prospect may not be responsive the first time, but as the relationship develops, be assured that the topic will come up again. Wealthy prospective clients will do business with people they like and trust, and as the personal relationship develops, the advisor in almost all cases will have the opportunity to expand that personal relationship to one of business, if they are prepared.

□   □   □

I have seen financial advisors become involved in nonprofits but not be successful in acquiring new affluent relationships or assets. Typically they are not following the lessons from the top advisors:

□ They do not become leaders within the organization.

□ They do not make clear to other nonprofit members what their occupation is.

□ They do not develop personal relationships with other nonprofit members.

□ They do not have transition lines prepared when the opportunity presents itself.

□ They are not patient enough to give this strategy time to work.

I strongly believe that people want to do business with others that they know and trust and have common interests with—and the nonprofit success principle provides the opportunity for that to happen. When I was a manager in Atlanta, I was asked to join the board of the Woodruff Arts Center, one of the most prestigious nonprofit boards in the city. I had the opportunity to interact with and develop relationships with the "Who's Who" of Atlanta. On the board, I was assigned the responsibility of contacting very affluent individuals who had made significant contributions to the performing arts in the past and asking them for contributions again. Often these requests were followed by an invitation to a high-profile dinner or event. It was the perfect opportunity to invite these donors to be my guest and begin to build a relationship with them. As these relationships developed, I had many opportunities to talk about investments, the markets, what my firm thought of the markets, and so on. If I had been an active financial advisor at the time and used the transition lines that I have outlined in this chapter, I am confident I could have turned many of these relationships into business.

NON-PROFIT ORGANIZATION INVOLVEMENT | 143

9

LESSON NINE

Long-Term Orientation

THE MAJORITY OF our top advisors started out with a simple vision: Survive first and, in the process, build a successful practice. As their businesses grew they all had to balance their own financial goals between the short and long term. A "product of the day" approach—where you focus on the sale of a particular product rather than an investment process—may help business in the short term, but it didn't always result in good performance for the client in the long term. Over time, our advisors were all able to transition to a long-term, comprehensive wealth-management approach, which will be described in Chapter 11.

First, however, this chapter covers the mindset that is needed to follow a long-term orientation approach to this business. Our top advisors learned to take a long-term perspective in most of their daily decisions, which meant investing money back into their business, being patient with prospects, doing marketing, and demonstrating their commitment to service. A long-term perspective also includes establishing a vision for your business. It means being proactive at working toward achieving a vision every day, rather than reacting to the crisis of the day. It's about building a quality-sustaining practice that will not only endure, but grow with time.

The difference between our top advisors and those who are less successful is not only the development of a vision, but a willingness to make the time and financial sacrifices that are often required to implement a long-term orientation mindset. For example, I know that it is difficult to market and execute an effective prospect list or "pipeline." Marketing is like exercise; in the short term it is hard to get started, but the long-term benefits outweigh the effort exerted.

Another aspect of long-term orientation is that the top advisors are not afraid to walk away from prospects that don't fit their business model or practice. Rather than accept the new relationship that would provide short-term income but long-term headaches, our top people might forgo a relationship because of their long-term orientation. It might be because of the prospects' personality, unrealistic expectations, or simply that their investment approach or style is too different. Adding additional clients that might provide short-term revenue but come with additional aggravation and conflict is not something our top advisors would accept.

With one exception, all our top advisors started with a transaction-based business in which they would charge a fee for each securities transaction. However, their businesses all evolved into a fee-based orientation, where they charge a fee not on each transaction, but rather as a percentage of assets. They learned that a fee-based business doesn't generate as much business as a transaction-based approach over the short term, but in the longer term it will contribute much more, because of the ongoing revenue stream. Because a fee-based structure is a percentage of assets, it is charged no matter how many or how few securities transactions take place.

At the same time, all of our top advisors follow a wealth-management approach to investing, which places the process ahead of a single investment and takes a long-term view based on a thoughtful plan. It takes a major commitment to interview each client and find out their goals, risk tolerance, and priorities; it also takes time to develop a plan on how these objectives will be reached. But spending this time sets the stage for a productive long-term relationship. Once again, you are demonstrating a long-term orientation as opposed to just investing client's assets without the wealth-management process.

Long-term orientation specifically relates to three important business strategies: client focus, marketing, and retained earnings.

Client Focus

The only way to create long-term, satisfied clients is to always put the client's interest first. Our top advisors all believe that in order to succeed they need to consistently do the right thing for their clients. Then the future takes care of itself, because satisfied clients lay the groundwork for uncovering more assets, gaining better referrals, and doing more overall business. I don't know whether they were each born with a strong moral compass or they developed it once they entered this business, but the fact is that each of them has one.

Putting the client's interest ahead of your own is considered a long-term approach to business because at times, short-term business opportunities must be left on the table in order to better serve the client. For example, often the best advice for a particular client is to do nothing with their money, or delay the purchase or sale of an investment. While this advice translates into a loss of commission in the short term, you are building a relationship of trust in the long term.

One of the hallmarks of a top advisor is the ability to pass up short-term business. Time after time, these advisors will tell a prospective client their honest opinion regarding whether their current portfolio is in good shape; they may recommend that no changes should be made. They'll offer a discounted rate to a good client even if they don't ask for it, waive their fee on a mortgage product to make the numbers work, and change from equities to cash and forgo the fees. Our top advisors willingly made these decisions because they know that in the long run, these actions show that they work from a position where the client's interests come first. They've also learned that in the world of money, giving up some for the benefit of someone else's gain is "priceless."

A trusting relationship is earned through actions, not words. Affluent clients both consciously and unconsciously test their relationship with their financial advisors. If the advisor passes the trust test, then they will have access to more of the client's assets and referrals, and the client's acceptance of most, if not all, of their recommendations. A trusting partnership is what our top advisors all strive for over the long term.

Top advisor Mike expresses his long-term orientation in the following way: "My thought has always been to figure out how to work best with a client so that I can be advising his or her family 25 years down the road. I know that this strategy leads to a different way of doing business, which affects how I make decisions, service my clients, and communicate with them. It is very different than someone looking to make a quick sale. In many ways, this strategy meant delaying success. It meant the sale might take a year, or it might take two years, because that was the right way to do it. But it results in a much higher-quality relationship that is going to be sustained."

Investing Time in Developing the Skills Your Prospects and Clients Have

David, another one of our top advisors, never liked golf, but knew he had to take it up for the benefit of his career. He told me, "For years I resisted playing golf because of the time it required, but eventually I realized it was the sport that many of my top referral sources and clients played. As a result I took it up." The same philosophy holds true with all of us. In order to put ourselves in the position to meet wealthy investors and develop relationships with them, we have to do what our target prospects and clients do. Whether it's fly-fishing, developing a taste for the performing arts, horseback riding, or going to the symphony, you should be willing to invest time in those activities because, in the long term, they'll pay off.

Marketing Focus

Marketing by its nature requires a long-term approach, but for marketing to work with the affluent, it takes even longer. All of the top advisors are committed to marketing as part of a long-term orientation. Several of them make direct marketing contact and are very effective at it; however, the majority of the top advisors take a more subtle approach.

Sam joined a prestigious country club before he could afford it; he learned to play golf, fly-fish, and hunt because in his market that was how he would meet wealthy investors. This was a very deliberate long-term strategy that required both a monetary and time commitment to put him in front of his potential affluent clients. This strategy worked for Sam: Over time, he assumed a leadership role at the country club and built social relationships which ultimately became clients.

As we've discussed, two of the most effective marketing strategies are building a professional referral network (Chapter 7) and joining nonprofit organizations (Chapter 8); both strategies require a long-term orientation. Success comes about when you build relationships with individuals who can have a positive impact on business.

Building an influencer network involves developing relationships with CPAs and attorneys that will refer wealthy investors to you. All the research indicates that this is the primary way that millionaires choose their financial advisor. However, it takes a long-term orientation for this approach to work. First, it takes time to develop the right relationships with influencers, and then it will take even longer before one actually starts to provide referrals. Many advisors attempt this strategy but fail because they don't spend enough time developing a professional and personal relationship with the influencer. The common practice is that they meet with the influencer, make a presentation, and expect referrals to come. In my research with CPAs, it takes at least 18 months of getting to know an advisor before these influencers feel comfortable making a referral to one of their clients.

A nonprofit marketing approach also requires patience. The cornerstone of this strategy is to assume a leadership position in a nonprofit organization in order to develop relationships with other affluent individuals involved in the group. In this way the advisor has access to wealthy individuals who would be hard to approach any other way. However, access is only the first step: Being a leader in the organization and earning the respect of the board members takes time. Personal relationships are developed through mutual respect and passion for the organization being served. It can take years to develop these partnerships and ultimately turn them into business relationships. But for the patient advisor, the opportunity to move from the personal relationship to a business one will come.

Retained Earnings

Our top advisors know that you need to spend money to make money. In fact, they all invest money back into their businesses. One of the biggest mistakes that I see advisors make is an unwillingness to spend on their own business. It takes a long-term orientation for advisors to invest in their businesses, but the top advisors recognize this investment is required to grow their practices.

For example, John started in the business when he was 26 years old, with no contacts, and 30 years later he is doing $7 million in business. John credits much of his success with his willingness to invest back into his own business. He hosts high-quality client dinners that are catered and feature the finest wines, all at his own expense. He also gives annual first-class client appreciation events that he pays for himself. John buys lunch for his team every day and funds any training expenses they incur.

How Much to Reinvest?

Anne probably expresses it best when asked how much money she reinvests in her business. Her answer is, "Whatever it takes." The average amount that our top advisors reinvest in their business expenses is 15 percent of their total compensation. The highest number was 20 percent of business generated, and the lowest was 10 percent. This total investment typically was divided as follows:

75 percent in employee payroll expenses

25 percent in travel, entertainment, and charitable expenses

As an example, if our top advisors generated $5 million in business and were paid $2.5 million, they would invest $250,000 back into their practice. Of the $250,000, they might spend approximately $185,000 in employee-related fees and $65,000 on travel, entertainment, and charitable expenses. According to our advisors, this percentage of retained earnings has remained constant through their careers. If you aspire to be a top advisor, you need to make the long-term commitments that the top advisors make. Developing a retained earnings budget of 10 percent of the business is a good place to start.

Implementing Lesson #9—A Case Study

My experience as a financial advisor was based on a long-term vision that incorporated many of these top advisor lessons, even though I didn't know them or their philosophies at the time. I wanted to become a million-dollar advisor, and while I had no clue how to do it, I understood that the right activities led to the right results. This case study incorporates many of the long-term lessons of this chapter.

The first step was setting long-term business goals and breaking those goals into annual, monthly, and weekly measurements. Some of these goals included new business generated, new assets brought in, new affluent clients acquired, and new prospects added to the prospect pipeline. Once they were set, I could plan out my daily activities that were needed in order to achieve my defined goals. I learned that keeping track of the activities and results was very important: I learned to believe in the motto, "You can't manage anything that you don't measure."

I then incorporated my niche focus into my long-term plan. My vision was that it would be easier to get appointments in smaller towns with wealthy individuals than the city I lived in. I started to implement my vision by visiting those towns every week in order to develop relationships with the community's affluent individuals and centers of influence. It took time and consistency before I could build a relationship of trust and begin to open new accounts. I also had to immerse myself into the selected town by reading the local paper, developing referral sources, speaking at the local civic clubs, joining the chamber of commerce, and contributing to the local charities. Once people in the targeted town knew I was committed to them and their community, my business grew exponentially.

In 1983, I teamed with another advisor in my office who was doing about the same level of business. We were one of the first teams in our region: Our manager thought we were crazy. Yet he allowed us to move forward, even though he knew that my partner and I had no idea how to create a team. Building a team required a vision and entailed risk, but both of us believed in the long-term benefit of working together. We discovered the value of brainstorming and sharing ideas and resources. Together we created a vision. We broke down our business and activity goals and held ourselves accountable.

We also realized that attracting and keeping a highly qualified sales assistant required investing money back in our business, and essential to the execution of our long-term plan. We convinced our manager to let us share an assistant; we paid part of her salary. She was so good that to keep her, we knew we would need to give her a bonus as well. All of these actions led to the desired results, and our business grew by 50 percent in our first full year as a team.

My partner and I also invested our own money in new technology. We bought an Apple IIe computer in 1983. Although it doesn't seem like a radical idea by today's standards, back then it was one of the first personal computers brought into our firm. It cost $5,000 at the time, which seemed like an enormous business expense, and required a long-term commitment to realize a profit from it. Yet this technology helped us track our clients and stay in touch with prospects in ways that differentiated us and contributed significantly to our business success.

I eventually became the manager of my office, but because it was a small office, the majority of my income came from my accounts. I realized it was too much to try to grow my practice, service my clients, and manage the office. So every year I purged my business of the smaller accounts and gave them to a new advisor. Many times these smaller clients did more business with their new advisor than they did with me. But I didn't look back and regret passing them on, because my vision was not in keeping with the size of these clients. And it worked. Despite working with fewer relationships, my business continued to grow. I took a short-term risk by giving away my small relationships, but it was essential to my long-term vision of working with more affluent investors and providing them with the service model they required.

I also joined the Kiwanis Club, a country club, the chamber of commerce, and my college alumni group. I became a jury commissioner, was active in my church, and moved my family to a nicer neighborhood. All of it took time and money, but they were the best investments that I could make. It took several years before this commitment paid off, but when it did, the payoff was significant. I was meeting all the right people and weaving myself into the fabric of my community. I was finally able to focus exclusively on affluent relationships, which was at the heart of my long-term vision.

My story is just one example of how adopting a long-term orientation mindset paid off. All of our top advisors have a similar story of how they developed a long-term vision for their businesses and worked toward that vision, investing the time and money required to turn their vision into reality.

10

Creating a Team

THE PROLIFERATION of teams in the financial services business has been a fairly recent phenomenon, gaining traction in the 1990s. With one exception, none of our top advisors had the opportunity to be a junior partner, because team opportunities simply didn't exist when most of them started. In many cases they were pioneers in the formation of teams in our industry. Yet every one of the top advisors told me that working with a team has given them the opportunity to spend more time doing what they do best: meeting with affluent clients and prospects. The team approach has universally made a positive difference in the success of their practices.

Today, every one of our top advisors is the leader of a vertical team structured to support the top advisor. The team structure enables the leader to do what they do best which is to build and develop client and prospective client relationships, to set the investment policy and processes, and to bring in new business. The rest of the team includes support staff and even other financial advisors who are considered junior partners in the business. As their businesses grew, all of our top advisors continued to recognize that they needed to attract and retain the "best" to support them. Therefore, they are very generous to their team members. Many of the senior associates make two to three times the compensation that a traditional firm would pay.

This high compensation is warranted because the cost of turnover is much higher than the generous compensation paid to proven team members. Losing someone means a disruption in client service and a loss of momentum for everyone. Most of the top advisors have at least one senior client associate that has been with them for many years, in some cases for over 20 years. This senior associate often serves as a chief of staff and has excellent relationships with clients. A high turnover rate is almost a way of life in financial services, but based on my experience, turnover occurs less often on our top advisors' teams. This is not only because of compensation, but also because of the pride of being part of a successful team.

John believes that one of the factors that accounts for his success is his team and their loyalty to him. "My senior associate has been with me for 23 years, and I have two other associates that have been part of my team for 15 and 10 years," he says. "Most of the people in my group joined me right out of college, so they grew up together and really enjoy working together. I believe I am only as good as the team that supports me."

As a rule, our top advisors are by many standards considered to be overstaffed. However, they all believe that it is money well spent. In their minds, it is impossible to overservice clients, and having the opportunity to delegate daily tasks is worth every dollar. Their teams evolved in many cases over a long period of time. For example, when I was John's manager, he was always suggesting that the company should pay for another client associate. When I did provide an additional assistant he would also hire a second, paying for that employee out of his own pocket.

Everyone Makes Hiring Mistakes

Just like anyone who hires people in any business, our top advisors have made mistakes in hiring. Choosing team members can be like choosing a spouse, and despite everyone's best intentions even supposedly good marriages don't always work. For instance, it is impossible to know in advance how well a new employee will gel with the rest of the team. For example, John was an early adopter of teams, yet over the years he has lost a number of staffers. Today, John has four members of his team who have more than ten years of experience with him, and his business continues to grow because his team works so well together.

Benefits of a Team Strategy

Being on a team as a financial advisor is no guarantee of success. However, if the elements of a successful team practice are in place, it will greatly increase the probability of achieving great financial results. The objective is to free up time for the team leader to do the work that he can't delegate. As discussed, this usually means working with the best clients and developing new relationships with high-net-worth prospective clients.

Our top advisors provide very specific job descriptions for all of their team members so that everyone has clearly defined responsibilities and knows what they are accountable for. Tasks can include:

❑ Administrative

❑ Client relationships

- Investment implementation
- Product specialties
- Client service
- Marketing

Sam puts it well when he offers the following advice: "Humility is an important virtue in this business. It's much better to build a strong team and then be able to talk about how good your team is to prospective clients, rather than focusing on how good you are. Your team can also position you in a positive way and build you up with clients and prospects in a way you can't do yourself."

Team Structure

Our top advisors all structured their teams differently. Some have junior partners that receive a minority split of the business; others have administrative support that receive supplemental compensation in addition to their salaries. However, they all have certain common elements: vertical positioning that supports the top advisor, and tenured team members who are well compensated.

More than half of our 15 top advisors retain a junior advisor partner. These junior partners usually came to their positions as the result of having some exposure to the top advisor, either personally or through working in the same office. They were either assigned, or the top advisor noticed them within the office and was attracted by their work ethic. In a few cases they were family members. The role of the junior partner is either to add to the marketing capacity or to serve as a client relationship manager, since both roles free up the top advisor to focus more on business development and the most profitable relationships.

Ross gives his partner enormous credit for moving the team in the direction of money in motion, with a focus on the executive market, which has taken their business to a new level. His partner developed the requisite expertise and worked aggressively to position Ross's team as a leader in these areas. The team's business has grown significantly as the result of the efforts of the junior partner, is very well compensated.

Sam's team includes himself and a partner. They split the proceeds of Sam's existing clients: 63 percent to Sam and 37 percent to his partner. All income from new business has been put into a 50/50 pool, and both partners have equal weight when it comes to providing and implementing the vision for the team to reach their goals. Sam and his partner spend about 10 percent of their income on supplemental income to the associates. They have three assistants to support the team: Two of the assistants divide the 60 clients equally, and one is responsible for just administrative duties. Sam ties his business model directly into his team structure, saying, "We have a client contact system that is based on monthly client contacts and face-to-face quarterly reviews. I'll pick topics for these meetings that we are going to follow. One of my assistants will put all the supporting documentation behind the agenda and what I should highlight. If I had to prepare it by myself, it wouldn't get done."

John spends between 10–15 percent of his earnings on team compensation. He has four client associates that service his 80 client relationships. Each is assigned specific investors, but every associate knows every one of John's clients. "The four client associates each have 20 accounts they work with directly, and they do everything for those clients. They develop deep relationships and really bond with them. If someone needs anything, an assistant handles it, they don't call me," John says. "So I am detached from client contact except for the monthly contacts and quarterly reviews." John also has two analysts on his team—one that provides presentation materials and another who prepares all the monthly and quarterly reviews. Additionally, John has a team member dedicated to his marketing efforts, including following up on his prospects.

Mike describes his team in the following way: "I run a vertical team and all the business goes through me. The analysts help manage the investment process. They focus on analyzing strategies and investment alternatives on the front end, and help make sure the assets are allocated according to the plan. They are responsible for generating our client performance reports, so the clients know how they are doing and also so they can be diagnostic, to figure out where we can make changes. My client associates take care of the administrative and service requirements of my clients."

Joseph spends 10 percent of his compensation for his team, and describes his business as a pyramid with him being the CEO. He has two junior partners who are in their 30s and share Joseph's philosophy of the business and how to manage money. They have their own production numbers and get about 10 percent each of the total business, leaving Joseph with 80 percent. They split all new business evenly and then adjust at the end of the year based on who has brought in what business. According to Joseph, "We have one client associate that takes care of our smaller accounts and the smaller end of our business. Then we have four client associates that are assigned our larger relationships. Each of these larger client relationships is assigned a lead associate, but all the support staff can cover for each other as needed."

David believes he still has phenomenal growth ahead of him, and the way he is going to get there is through his team structure. David currently has two client associates. One of them does all the administrative work, scheduling travel, maintaining his calendar, and servicing his clients. The other associate prepares the performance reviews, helps with the portfolio structure, and works with some clients. David wants to add at least one additional person to further enhance the servicing of his clients, enabling him to spend more time on business development. While he delegates most tasks, he remains responsible for strategizing on investment ideas, saying, "I have to be prepared to provide good investment ideas that are going to offer value to my clients."

Rob's team manages $1.4 billion in assets for 78 client relationships; his minimum client size is $10 million. Rob spends 10 percent of his earnings for out-of-pocket expenses, and about 75 percent of that is for team compensation above what his firm pays. Rob is the face of the organization to close business and present proposals. The team's investment strategy is his responsibility. He has a team of six, including himself and his junior partner, two analysts, and two client associates. His partner is in charge of implementing investment strategy and administration. His analysts are responsible for proposal building, investment research, and analysis. Two associates are interchangeable in servicing the clients.

Anne has one partner that she splits the business with in a 75/25 percent arrangement. An analyst handles all the fixed-income investments for the team, and there are two client associates. Because of Anne's expertise in executives and corporate services, she has developed a second team that handles relationships that are below her minimum. Such clients come her way as an offshoot of her corporate business; typically these relationships are less than $5 million. This second team has two advisors and one assistant, and she splits the business from clients she has given them 50/50. Anne is the only one on her team that actively markets; she alone is responsible for the strategy and planning for their top clients. Associates are responsible for the partner's schedule and client service and are trained to cover for each other. Her team works with 62 relationships with assets of $1.3 billion. She retains 20 percent of her earnings for business expenses and spends 75 percent of that on team compensation.

Ross and his partner spend about 10 percent of their earnings on their business, and 70 percent of their retained earnings are spent on supplemental compensation for their associates. The team works with 120 clients and $1.3 billion in assets. Ross's team consists of a junior partner and two client associates. He divides the business with his partner as follows: The first $2 million is split 70/30; from $2 million to $3 million the split is 60/40; and above $3 million it is 50/50. The split last year averaged out to be 66/34. The reason that the first $2 million is split 70/30 is because Ross regularly did $1.5 million in business before his partner joined the team. When the partner initially joined, Ross told him, "I'm going to overpay you early in your career and you're going to overpay me later in my career." Ross meant that eventually he would work less but still be expected to be paid well by the younger partner.

The rest of Ross's team includes one client associate who focuses on the administrative side, and a senior associate whose primary responsibility is problem solving and service. Each associate has a different expertise with the different products the team offers their clients. For example, one associate has an expertise in restricted stock, another one lending. Ross explains how the client associates work: "Both are responsible for service, and will take whatever client calls come in. In some instances, both might actually talk to the same client: One might be working on a mortgage and then transfer to the other, to follow up on an operational problem."

Jack has two advisor partners on his team that he splits business with 60/30/10. Jack is the quarterback and works with one of his partners (his son) on business development. The 10 percent partner focuses on the structure and rules of retirement plans, lending, and insurance. The 30 percent partner has a strong orientation on the equity side of the business, while Jack is more balanced between equities and bonds. Jack works with about half the client relationships, typically the largest ones, and divides the rest as follows: The 10 percent partner handles the smaller relationships, and the 30 percent partner takes on the balance. Jack brings in the 30 percent partner whenever he brings in a new relationship, and the new client appreciates getting to know both advisors from the beginning. The team has two client associates, and one works primarily with Jack and his clients and the other associate works with the two junior partners.

Jack describes the interaction of partners as follows: "We have steady contact with each other and, as a result, don't have formal meetings. I've observed different teams that seem like they are holding hands and meeting all the time. We don't do that. We interact throughout the day asking each other's opinions about things."

William Runs His Business Like a Doctor's Office

William has a vertical team with three client associates. One of the associates does all of the analytics, the credit products, and insurance. Another associate is licensed and enters all of his trades. These two associates service the clients and get the client reviews ready for William. He also has a part-time associate to do clerical work, to lighten the load of the associates. He describes his team in the following way:

> "I have built my practice around the doctor's model. When you go into a doctor's office, you walk into the exam room and somebody else comes in and they ask you about your symptoms; they fill out the chart, they take your blood pressure, your temperature, and prep you for the doctor. Then they put your file in a rack on the door, and there are seven doors in the hallway, all with patients waiting. When it's your turn the doctor walks in, grabs the chart off the door, and spends 30 seconds looking at it before meeting with you.

> "When clients come to see me in my office, the appointment goes much the same way. I'll review Mr. Smith's file for about five minutes while he is having a cup of coffee with someone on my staff. My team has prepared his review so that it's ready for me to spread out on my table. I understand what I want to

do; I look at the asset allocation, I look for positions we are no longer using or things I want to switch. Then we bring him back to meet with me. And I didn't schedule that review, I didn't send out the reminder for it, I didn't print any of the paperwork, I didn't prep it. For me, the ability to do one review every hour for six hours straight and not to have to do any prep, that's the only way you can do that volume. I know people who only do two or three reviews a week and they think that's a big deal. We do six a day."

William doesn't want to lose any affluent clients and realizes the importance of proactive service in high client retention. His long-term plans include adding another associate whose main job will be improving customer service so that existing clients won't leave the practice, "because when I look at the gap in my practices, it's providing more proactive service rather than reacting," William says. "The front door is wide open. Through September we added 11 new affluent clients this [past] year, while our firm's average is only two. I have taken the front door off the hinges by bringing in a lot of new affluent relationships. Yet I'm still concerned about losing clients through the back door."

Implementing Lesson #10

The first step to implementing this principle is to look at your current business model and structure. If you are not part of an existing team, ask yourself if you currently have enough support so that you can focus on relationship building with existing clients, business development, and providing your best clients with world-class service. If not, I would strongly suggest that you consider hiring one client associate or splitting the cost with another highly motivated advisor who is willing to invest in a team. In many cases, this expense is going to be in addition to the client associate salaries paid by your firm.

If you are part of an existing team, compare your current structure and practices with the practices of the top advisors, and determine if any changes need to be made. Even if you are not the senior member of a team, or if your group is not a vertical organization, you can still incorporate many of the following best team practices.

Six Elements of a Successful Team

As I've said, a team is like a marriage, and many of the elements of a successful marriage apply to a successful team. The most important elements of a successful team are having the right fit and the same commitment level, and sharing a common vision and goals. Once those success elements are in place, taking the team to the next level involves six important practices, which can apply whether or not the team is vertically structured.

❑ *Shared Values.* The core values should be established by the team leader, then shared with the rest of the team, and followed by all. Important team values can include the client experience, how members of the team are compensated and recognized, and how portfolios are invested. The team leader needs to clearly communicate to all members of the team, especially new members. A lack of team values, or the lack of communication of these values, will result in inevitable problems, as not all team members will act in accordance with these values and a disconnect among team members will result.

❑ *Vision.* All team members are better and more productive when they are working toward specific goals and a vision. The vision doesn't have to stay the same—in fact, it should be flexible and fine-tuned over time. The most important factor is that there is a team vision with specific short- and long-term goals that the team leader must develop and articulate for the team. My past experience has shown that advisors who have specific goals do better than those who don't.

❑ *Accountability.* Once the vision and values have been established and communicated, every member of the team must be held accountable for their role in reaching the goals and achieving the vision of the business. A high level of accountability serves as a powerful motivator and will increase the focus and productivity of every team member.

A job description should be written for each team member that outlines what that person is responsible for. Compensation and recognition should be based on the contributions each individual team member makes in his or her area of responsibility. At regular intervals, team members should share their results as compared to their long-term goals. This process provides the needed accountability.

❑ *Frequent and Open Communication.* Good communication is essential to any team venture. The most frequent problems I have observed in teams—and the easiest to remedy—are communication problems. Teams must establish venues for communication and foster open and candid dialogue. I recommend that teams have an hourly meeting once a week. Use an agenda to keep the meeting focused and on track. The meeting can reinforce values, vision, accountability, and provide an opportunity for team members to contribute new ideas. Time should be set aside during each meeting for brainstorming and an open discussion to share ideas about what can make the team better. In addition, the senior partner should have an open-door policy and encourage team members to feel comfortable sharing their concerns, issues, and ideas.

❑ *Fair Compensation.* Compensation must be fair to all parties for a team to be effective. As the team grows, those responsible for the growth must be compensated for their contributions. This is particularly true with the less senior partners. Junior partners want to participate in the growth of the business with the hope of achieving parity in the future. If successful, high potential advisors are limited to a small percentage of the practice they will become frustrated and could end up leaving. Accountability and compensation must go hand in hand for the team to be effective. Recognition can be as important as compensation, especially for client associates. One of the positive aspects of a team is that members are working for a higher cause than just themselves. Recognition reinforces and motivates people to give the extra effort.

❑ *Succession Plan.* The retirement of a senior partner is inevitable, and as a result a succession plan needs to be developed and communicated to all clients, as well as to the members of the team. Many senior advisors are uncomfortable with a succession plan because they worry that circumstances might change in the future. Yet, by not communicating a strategy, the other partners don't know where they stand and what their stake in the partnership will be. This uncertainty can become an ongoing distraction that affects morale and loyalty.

A succession plan can be changed and refined over time with the team's input, but there should always be one in place. The succession plan gives all a clear view of their roles in the team's future, and it can serve as a positive motivator in ensuring every team member is committed to long-term success.

❑　❑　❑

After reading this chapter, it may seem unrealistic for your existing business to be able to support teams as large as those of our top advisors. The important thing to remember is that you don't need to have a mega-team in order to be successful, but you will need to have the right level of support so that your business can grow. Developing a team to support your efforts costs money, but as our top advisors have found out, it is one of the best investments they can make.

11

Wealth Management

WEALTH MANAGEMENT is a comprehensive and holistic investment process that integrates the long-term goals of an individual with financial solutions, using a planning-based and consultative approach. Wealth managers focus on understanding the client first, and spend whatever time is necessary to do that before the first investment is made. Many advisors don't spend the time to really understand their clients' goals and dreams, or their risk tolerance. They do not incorporate these vital pieces of information into a comprehensive plan designed to achieve goals within a specific risk parameter. At the same time, wealth managers can offer a variety of different financial products and services that are all related to the clients' total financial situation, such as banking services, liability management, mortgages, asset protection, estate planning, or philanthropic services.

Our top advisors go far beyond merely buying and selling investments. Instead, they view themselves as wealth managers. They are all committed to investing their time in the beginning of a business relationship to gain a deep understanding of their client's mindset, risk tolerance, past experience, and long-term goals. By understanding their client's "fears" and "dreams," they can put together a customized investment plan to achieve their client's goals. This discovery process enables advisors to inform their clients from the beginning on whether the clients' goals are reasonable, given their tolerance of risk. If their financial goals are not reasonable, it gives advisors the opportunity to educate their clients on the dynamics of risk and reward, so the advisor can give a client the right perspective and expectations. Yet many of the advisors in our industry do not take this approach.

Developing a formal document that systematically lays out the investment plan is another important aspect of the wealth-management process. The value of the plan is that it takes the intangible process of investments and makes it real. The client can read it, understand it, refer back to it, and share it with other advisors (a CPA and/or estate attorney, for example) and family members. It also is very important for the advisor so that she can reference the plan during quarterly reviews and put the investment performance into a long-term context.

But wealth management actually goes beyond the client's investments. The goal of every wealth manger is to be the "quarterback" of their client's entire financial life. This work extends to estate planning, lending, insurance, retirement, and educational planning. By discussing all aspects of the client's financial life during the discovery and planning process, top advisors position themselves as individuals uniquely capable of tying everything together in one comprehensive plan. This approach appeals to affluent clients because having one advisor to coordinate all aspects of their financial life simplifies what can be a very complex process.

Each advisor might not be an expert on all of the noninvestment aspects of a client's financial picture, but the advisor can assemble a team of experts to be brought in as needed. This team can be created from within a financial services firm using internal specialists, or it can be assembled by bringing in outside experts. Advisors need to do their due diligence in assembling a team of qualified and experienced estate planning attorneys, insurance specialists, bankers, and CPAs. Once a team is assembled, the advisor is in the position to be the quarterback on all aspects of the client's financial life.

By taking this type of comprehensive approach, our top advisors found that their business and assets increased while client retention improved. Better still, I have found that the advisors who offered the widest variety of investment products and services were able to increase their business exponentially. I have observed that almost perfect retention occurs when an affluent client has need for six or more different financial products and services. Examples of these could include (in addition to the primary investment account) a separate account for business and banking, life insurance, mortgages, home equity loans, trust services, a health savings account, a 529 college savings plan, online bill paying, direct deposit service, long-term health care, and credit and debit cards. Additionally, as discussed in the chapter on relationship building, my experience indicates that the easiest assets an advisor will ever get are those that clients have held away. The first step in acquiring these held-away assets is to find out about them, which is accomplished during the discovery and planning meeting during the first step of the wealth-management process.

A Win-Win Situation

The wealth-management approach is a classic "win-win" situation for both client and advisor. All of the advisors interviewed for this book have evolved into wealth managers as they discovered that this is the way affluent clients want to do business. The attractiveness of the wealth-management approach to millionaires is validated by a study done by Russ Alan Prince and shared in his book, *Cultivating the Middle-Class Millionaire*. Prince discovered that 77 percent of millionaires preferred to work with wealth managers. Prince's definition of a wealth manager is one who is "taking a comprehensive, holistic approach in order to provide integrated solutions." Prince surveyed more than 500 financial advisors and discovered that only 8.4 percent of them fit this description. Most of the advisors surveyed were investment generalists (79 percent) who described themselves as "offering a broad range of investment products but do not have a comprehensive planning orientation."

Our top advisors have capitalized on this gap between the wealthy investor's needs and what is available in the financial services marketplace. In a highly competitive industry, providing a differentiation that is attractive to the buyer makes the difference between success and failure.

The following are some of the many benefits of the wealth-management approach:

◻ More business comes in. When clients increase the number of different investment products and services they use, your business increases exponentially.

◻ Retention significantly increases with an expansion of investment products and services, as well as the regular proactive contact that is part of the wealth-management process.

◻ Asset discovery from existing clients leads to acquisition of those assets.

◻ This process incorporates the clients' other advisors, which can lead to the development of professional referred sources.

◻ Affluent clients prefer to work with wealth managers rather than investment generalists, giving the wealth manager an advantage in a highly competitive industry.

The Wealth-Management Process

The process of wealth management requires a substantial investment on the part of the financial advisors that embrace it. There are no shortcuts to becoming an effective wealth manager, but the rewards, as our top advisors have discovered, are well worth the time. They must invest in their professional development to achieve a level of expertise that clients who want to be advised require regarding all aspects of their financial lives. The financial advisor must understand the markets and be able to interpret them for their clients, while investing the portfolios through a long-term, disciplined process. They must invest the time to understand the risk tolerance level of their clients and develop an asset allocation strategy that is consistent with the clients risk tolerance. They must invest time in the discovery process and develop a plan before any investments are made. They also must invest time in assembling a team of experts that can be brought in to help them provide the comprehensive approach that wealth management requires. Additionally, they must follow up on a regular basis to review and update the plan.

The top advisors followed the wealth-management process, but like every other success principle they implemented, they did it their own way. While there are common practices, there are also differences. Some of the top advisors were more formal in the wealth-management process than others. For example, John's plans are very detailed and formally presented, with lots of charts and graphs. Joseph chooses to create a more loosely structured plan for every client.

The creation of a financial plan, regardless of the level of formality, is the first step in the process. It allows advisors to ask personal questions and discuss the client's goals, dreams, and risk tolerance. I believe you could uncover 50 percent or more of the assets that are held away just by doing a complete profile on a client and updating that information every year. As top advisor Jack states, "You would be amazed at how much of the assets of clients in the top half of the book you don't have. You have to ask questions like, How much do you owe? What is your income? How much do you spend and save? How many total assets do you have, and where are they? What financial responsibilities do you have for children and parents?"

Jack then positions himself to be an essential member of his client's team. That means giving his clients full access to him 24/7. He encourages people to call him at home, and he is willing to meet on weekends. His philosophy is that if his clients have a problem, he wants to know about it. In his view, he plays an important role in helping to ensure that his clients don't outlive their wealth, which means doing a reality check with them on their spending habits (are they living within their means?) and being realistic about their investment returns.

David's objective is having the complete trust of his clients so that he can oversee and handle every aspect of their financial lives. That is the only way he would enter into a client relationship; he doesn't want to be a small part of their overall financial situation. He believes that would be a waste of his capabilities and a disservice to his clients. In David's words, "I have found my wealthy clients want me to immerse myself in their financial lives, and I expect those clients to pay a reasonable fee for that [service]. I feel that I know more about investment management than any client that I'm interfacing with. If you're not in it—if you're not doing [wealth management] day to day and thinking it through—you don't really know this business. It's hard for people that are not doing it every day; this is not easy stuff that we do."

William shares a story that illustrates the power of the wealth-management approach and why it is so appealing to wealthy investors. William was once referred to a $10 million prospect who was going to interview three teams. William didn't know what the others said, but he suspects they talked about their past investment performance. However, William took the time to review the prospect's information in advance of his presentation and found that he had a living trust done, but it wasn't included on any of his documents. Additionally, nothing was titled in the trust and no beneficiaries were named. William told the prospect, "You know, I didn't bring any investments to talk about because it doesn't matter; this is all going to taxes anyway because what you tried to do is not going to happen. If you are with me, we are going to sweat the small details first and then we'll worry about what investments to do." William beat his competition and got the account.

Sam coordinates with his client's other advisors, including their tax advisors, as part of his services. He also takes the time to speak with his client's children, and with the client's spouse. Sam tells me, "If a client dies and the kids take control, where is it going to go? You better have a relationship with the kids." To Sam's point, in my experience as a manager, I have frequently seen large accounts transferred away from advisors when a client dies because the advisor did not invest the time to establish relationships with their client's children. Subsequently, there is no loyalty to their parent's advisor.

Joseph Provides a Vast Range of Services

Joseph closes at least 75 percent of the people going through this process with him. Because he wants his clients to come to him for everything they do financially, it is not uncommon for his clients to ask him if they can afford a new car or whether they should remodel their house. So Joseph starts every client relationship with a planning-based approach, although he puts more value on the execution than the sophistication of the plan. For example, when Joseph meets with a prospect for the first time, he describes the process as follows:

"I want to hear about everything that they do, and everything is important. I ask, 'What else is important to you?' I ask 'what else' in the first meeting at least a half dozen times. I get so much information asking 'what else.' Finally, when they say, 'Well, I can't think of anything else,' [then] I've got the information I need.

"At the first meeting, one of the things I tell people is that I am not the right guy for everybody, but when we are the right fit, we do really valuable work for our clients. So what I want to do is to find out if we are right for each other. After we talk about what is important to the client in terms of their life and their finances, then I share some of our methodology and write up a formal course of action. Based on this discovery meeting and the ensuing plan, they can decide if I'm a good fit or not.

"By the next meeting I have developed a list of everything we have talked about. I say, 'Here are the things that I understood are important to you,' and I have them listed, usually [as issues] 1–17, and people will be astonished that we were able to write down 17 things, so they will end up saying, 'Wow, we didn't realize we had all those issues.'" Then I say, here is what we would recommend, and as we share our recommendations we connect them to their issues. When we are done with our recommended course of action we have addressed every goal. Most of these recommendations include investments, estate planning, and insurance issues.

"After going through this process we ask for feedback: Did they like our approach? What are their thoughts? Based on their response and enthusiasm, we will either encourage them to sign the paperwork and open an account, or encourage them to give some thought to the course of action recommended and to set up a follow-up meeting within the next week, and then we can iron out any differences and decide if they are interested in working with us."

The way our top advisors invest money is less of a differentiator than the wealth-management process. In his book *Breaking Through*, John Bowen expresses this point very well when he writes: "So much academic research has been done on investment methodology and asset allocation that most advisors are doing a sound job with their client's investments. We might argue about the last 5 percent of how to manage our client's money, but 95 percent of the solution is clearly visible and available to any advisor willing to use it."

A Conservative Approach

Our top advisors all use a conservative approach to investing their client's assets. They have learned by working with more and more affluent investors that preservation of wealth is more important than exposing clients to unnecessary risks for higher returns. For example, Joseph believes it is more important how you do in a bad market than a good market. John shares this philosophy of using a conservative approach when investing client's assets. "If I can change one thing in my career," John says, "it would have been taking less risk [with] clients' money and being more risk-adverse. My clients are much more affluent now than during the early years of my career, and my main objective is trying to preserve their wealth, not taking a lot of risk to get them a high return."

Mike also takes a very conservative approach to investing his clients' money. He describes his approach to investing as follows: "We are looking to optimize risk-adjusted returns with a significant focus on risk management. All of our clients are already wealthy, so it is our job to keep them wealthy first and foremost and then grow their wealth at an acceptable rate over time. We spend a tremendous amount of time focused on diversification and the quality of investments that we use. If I summarized our investment process in a few words, it would be diversification, diversification, and diversification."

Anne shares her conservative investment approach, saying, "I think the biggest risk to our clients is that inflation is going to erode their ability to pass their wealth on three generations from now, so that's where our growth model comes in. Most of our clients don't need any more money to meet their own life objectives." Anne is very process-based with her investment approach. "Everything has a process," she says. "I am very disciplined about following my asset allocation strategy, and I make sure that I review and reallocate funds regularly to keep the allocation consist with the strategy. I also have a backup plan for each process: I make sure that the team monitors each client's asset allocation and ensures it is consistent with the plan. We don't want any surprises. I know that I have an amazing responsibility, and we are committed to doing it well."

Implementing Lesson #11

The implementation of the wealth manager's success principle starts with the understanding of the wealth-management process. The following is a summary of each of the steps:

◻ *Discovery and Planning Meeting.* This initial meeting is the essential first step of the wealth-management process. Through an extensive interview, the advisor discovers the client's or potential client's financial goals, risk tolerance, and past investment experience. A review of related financial documents is also recommended, including recent banking statements, tax returns, estate plans, insurance policies, and mortgage or loan documents.

◻ *Development of a Plan.* The advisor then takes the information obtained through the discovery meeting and develops a written plan that is designed to achieve the client's financial goals. This plan should be consistent with the client's risk tolerance. This plan can be either formal or informal, depending on the advisor's preference, but it should be a written plan. It is recommended that a Monte Carlo analysis be done to determine the probability of the recommended investment strategy in reaching the client's financial goals.

Recommendations should include liability, estate planning, and insurance strategies when appropriate. The best stocks, bonds, funds, and managers are identified, screened, and selected in advance to be used for the investment portion of the plan.

❐ *Plan Review.* The advisor sets up a second meeting to review the plan with the client and the client's spouse. This meeting should provide an overview of the plan, including how (if followed) it will reach the investor's goals. Other advisors working with the client, including CPAs and estate attorneys, can be invited to this plan review session.

❐ *Plan Implementation.* Once the client has been secured and the plan agreed upon by all parties, the advisor begins the process of asset allocation and investment selection. There must be a disciplined process for determining what equities and bonds will be bought, and what managers or funds are to be used. When appropriate, alternative investments should be considered for the portfolio as well. The development of an investment matrix is recommended for each investment class and size and style. Other implementation steps could include the development or update of an estate plan, the addition of insurance coverage or replacement of existing policies, and credit and mortgage reviews (for refinancing or replacement of credit lines when appropriate). In most cases these noninvestment products and services should be decided on in conjunction with the advisor's team of specialists.

❐ *Plan Performance Reviews.* The advisor needs to contact the client on a regular basis to review the plan and make appropriate changes. These reviews should be done formally every quarter and reallocation of assets should be recommended during each quarterly review, when appropriate. The performance of the portfolio should also be reviewed in the context of the plan and potential changes recommended.

□ *Annual Plan Update.* The annual update should be a more extensive plan review. In addition to receiving an investment recap, the client should be asked about assets held away and referral opportunities. The annual update is also an opportunity to do a service review, verify the client's goals and risk tolerance, and reexamine the noninvestment parts of the plan.

Maintaining Client Contact Is Key

Once the wealth-management steps are built into the advisor's practice, monthly contact with clients is a necessary ingredient to the wealth-management process. In my experience reviewing hundreds of client satisfaction surveys, client contact is the number-one factor influencing client retention. Affluent clients want proactive contact from their advisors, and once a month appears to be the "sweet spot."

If you have 100 total client relationships, then you'll be making five proactive client contacts a day in order for all of your clients to be contacted once a month. These monthly contacts are inclusive of the quarterly and annual reviews. Not only will these monthly contacts result in good client relationships, but they will also give you the opportunity to leverage client goodwill and to pursue marketing and asset-gathering opportunities. The structure of these monthly contacts is reviewed in detail in Chapter 16.

12

Commitment to Service

OUR TOP ADVISORS all recognize that having what Kenneth Blanchard calls "raving fan" clients is instrumental to their success. Raving fans are loyal, affluent clients who provide significantly more referrals, bring in more assets, and do much more business than just "satisfied" clients. To increase the number of raving fan clients, our top advisors are all committed to providing a very high level of service. In fact, our top advisors are fanatical about client service. When asked about their service model, time after time they responded that their business was about delivering "flawless service." Sam believes that in many instances, service can be more important than performance. "A reasonable investment return is expected, but service in many cases can be the differentiation," he says.

The success principle of service is very closely linked to the principles of long-term orientation, "leverage of size," teams, and the wealth-management process. As you begin to work with wealthier clients, you'll see that your client's expectations for excellent service are very high, and if you don't deliver your relationship with them is at risk. Because of this dynamic, all our top advisors recognize the importance of building a strong service model into their practice.

The challenge that any advisor who works with highly affluent clients faces is how to meet the high expectations these affluent clients have for service. For example, Anne has a very affluent client base and her approach to service reflects her commitment to them. "It's our number-one priority," she says. "We work with people who are very powerful within their companies, and they are used to everybody jumping at their immediate request. So, we are going to do that, too. I am always overstaffed, which is counterintuitive to most businesses. I always have capacity on my team, so I have more personnel than I need right now. As soon as I feel everyone is at full capacity I will hire someone else, because I believe service is so important." Anne adds that "our clients are giving us responsibility, in most cases, for 100 percent of their wealth; one mistake is one too many, and the only way to avoid that is to have processes and then a check of those processes at all times."

The cornerstone of a strong service model is always putting the client first, which requires long-term orientation. If clients know that you are committed to them, then they will be loyal. Your team also ensures that you can provide excellent service: Our top advisors have developed their teams to offer the affluent deeper levels of service. This means that they have developed their infrastructure so that they have enough time to provide frequent and consistent contact with clients. The frequency that seems best is once a month. Some clients require more and some require less, but the experience of most top advisors is that a proactive monthly contact is the "sweet spot." This commitment limits the number of client relationships that an advisor can effectively work with.

All team members must have a similar commitment to service as the aspiring top advisor; everyone must share the vision of the client being the most important priority of their job. If there is a weak link in the chain, the service experience will suffer. Our top advisors instilled this mindset into their team members and took responsibility to make sure they were trained to provide that level of experience.

Finally, the wealth-management approach is integral to the client service experience because the more comprehensive the relationship between the advisor and client, the more satisfied the client will be. Our top advisors have found that if their clients need a broad range of products and services that they can provide, it cements their relationship over the long term. One industry retention study supported this approach, showing that affluent clients with six or more different products and services have a 99 percent retention rate with their advisor.

Proactive Service Pays Off

The biggest difference in the service model of our top advisors, as compared to those who are less successful, is being proactive. My experience shows that most advisors react to client problems instead of positioning themselves in front of them. Our top advisors have found that to attract and keep wealthy clients, providing proactive high-touch service is a requirement.

Providing proactive service means anticipating your clients needs before they do, and our top advisors recognize that the single most important factor in client satisfaction is proactive contact between themselves and their clients. It gives the affluent client the sense that the advisor and the advisor's team are in control of matters and have the time to provide exceptional service. All the client surveys indicate that the reason most clients leave an advisor is that they don't hear from their advisor enough. This is validated by my own experience. When I would make follow-up contact with any large clients transferring their accounts to another firm, in most cases, clients would indicate that their reason for leaving was because they never heard from their advisor.

Mike describes his business as proactive, and believes that is what makes it stand out: "I don't like to react. I like to be proactive. We are usually out in front of things, bringing things to our clients' attention. It's our initiative that I believe makes a difference. It gives us the ability to be more thoughtful and focused."

Such service is also a cornerstone of Sam's business model. According to Sam, "Our client associates all make proactive service calls. Our team has a monthly meeting to identify potential issues in advance. Examples could include letting our clients know that a K-1 tax report from a particular portfolio has been mailed or is online for them to view. Another example is to let them know their year-end tax reporting statement has just been sent, and [asking] would they like us to send a copy to their CPA. We want to make proactive service calls when we anticipate a potential issue, and actively contact our clients before they contact us."

Ross describes his client contact process as follows: "We use a computer-based client contact program that organizes our client contacts monthly. Before we finish any conversation or review with them, we schedule their next monthly contact, much like making a doctor's appointment."

Joseph talks to every client at least monthly. His staff gives him a list of clients names every week so he can make the calls. "Every time I talk to a client I give them a market update and ask how they are doing. We meet personally with all of our best clients twice a year, which is a formal review," Joseph says.

William is committed to monthly contact calls, and during these contacts he asks the following questions: "Is there any statement problem or issues that are unresolved? Is there anything on your mind that we can help you with? Are we meeting your service expectations?"

David actually meets with his clients quarterly rather than calling them monthly. "My clients know they are going to see me once a quarter, if they like it or not. They know we are going to discuss performance, that we are going to discuss every aspect of the strategy, and they look forward to the meetings," he says. "However, based on the market conditions, we may make some changes throughout the quarter."

Excellent Service Means Something Different to Everyone

While all the top advisors are committed to providing excellent service to their clients, their tactics and methodologies are different. For example, Joseph prefers to treat his clients "royally." In his words, "When clients come in the door, the team is committed to treating them like they are the most important [people] in the world. If a client wants something that is quirky or out of the ordinary, our team is there to deliver it. The team is there so [our clients] don't get frustrated with issues they need resolved."

John believes that the core of a great service experience is a well-trained team: "If someone calls our office they never get voice mail. They are going to reach a highly trained, quality person. Everyone on our team knows all of our clients. When we hire new [staff], we put them through an extensive training program, so they really learn our processes and clients. When they start, one of their first jobs is to put together the quarterly reviews so that they understand how portfolios are made up and get an inside view of each client. I encourage all our team members to have a professional designation, which I pay for."

Anne shares John's philosophy on the importance of her team in providing a high level of service to her clients. "My team members are intelligent, they are quick, they are responsive," she says, "and

[they] are definitely owners in the business, so they have every reason to want to make sure that these clients are serviced as much as
I do. My team executes the tactics of our client service model. I am
a big picture person, and when there is work to do I just want it
done. I don't really want to share in how my team is going to make
it happen. I get involved if something goes wrong and help fix it, if
I'm needed. We are always trying to improve and talk about how we
can get better and make sure that problems are anticipated and,
when in our control, don't occur again."

Rob shares some examples of the service he provides. "If I'm out of
the office a client will never hear, 'I can't help you; he's out of the
office.' Problems are taken care of no matter where I am because it is
either handled [by the team] or a call is made to me, and I provide the
answer and it gets done. We have no distinction between A, B, or C
clients; if they are one of our 78 clients, they get first-class service,"
he says. Rob's team can solve most problems immediately, and he gives
this example: "If a client says that they want to give a donation to the
Museum of Science, within ten minutes the client associate looks at
the appreciated positions to determine the best position to donate,
informs the client, and then takes care of the logistics of the donation."

William believes he has drifted away from providing the high level
of service that he once did, saying, "The service we provided used to
be better than it is now. When we got a new client we would do a
statement binder for them and have a separate meeting to teach them
how to read their statements. My goal is to get back to providing a
great service experience for our affluent clients, and that is what the
new associate I plan to hire will be in charge of. This client associate
will provide proactive service calls and ask, 'Is there any statement
problem or issues that are unresolved? Is there anything inaccurate or
missing? What can we help you with? Do you need to speak to
William for any reason?'"

According to Ross, it is especially important to make the initial
client experience a very positive one, so his team puts a lot of effort

and time into the relationship in the beginning. Once the relationship is set up, he finds that it requires less time. He also tries to tailor the service to the needs of individual clients. Ross gives an example of the kind of service his team offers: "We had a client who donates back to his alma mater, Dartmouth, every year. Every year he doesn't have to call us because one of our associates has already sent him the form and all he does is put in the number of shares and signs it. He doesn't know how we do it."

Greg Provides Flawless Service

Greg believes that offering his clients the highest level of service is a requirement:

> "Any client that works with us will have a flawless experience on the administrative side of the business. So when clients come in, they know that they are in a professional environment. Everyone here is trained and has the ability to deal with our clients in the most professional manner. My clients love my client associate; she handles everything, and they send her gifts. It starts with opening up the account, wiring funds, replacing lost credit cards, and dealing with the financial side of gifts, education, death, or illness of our clients and their families.
>
> "Now the investment side is much grayer: I wish the investment side was as flawless."

Greg believes he should be accessible to his clients whenever they need him. "I am available 24/7," he says, "and with e-mail, everyone takes advantage of that. I got an e-mail last Sunday night at 10:47 p.m. It was a question on setting up a specific type of retirement account. I responded to her 30 seconds later, saying that we will research it in the morning and get back to her first thing Monday. She e-mailed me back saying, go to sleep, you have become a Blackberry addict. And she's right."

Greg shares another story of how his commitment to service paid off:

"Our manager gave us a relatively small account. We called the client and later sent a letter because we could not reach them. One day we received a frantic call from the client's wife because her husband was away on a business trip and she needed some money wired. My assistant handled the situation promptly and sent the money out. The client was very happy about how we handled the situation. When her husband came back from his business trip, he talked to his wife about how well her requests had been handled and saw the letter I had sent, and said he was not aware that our firm had all of these services to offer. That wound up eventually becoming a $25 million relationship."

Implementing Lesson #12

Every sports enthusiast understands that without a strong defense, even the greatest offense will fail. In developing a top advisor financial practice, it is just as important to have a world-class service model as it is to have a world-class client acquisition model. The awareness of the importance of this dynamic really came to my attention when my firm put together an incentive program for the acquisition of new relationships. Many of our advisors reached the level of acquiring four new affluent relationships in a 12-month period. But the incentive was based on the net number of new relationships: acquired clients minus lost clients. Only a relatively small number of advisors won the incentive because of the "net" requirement. This meant that on the whole, clients were not provided with the level of customer service needed to retain them.

A superior service model starts with having a manageable number of client relationships. As the affluence of your clients increases, you will discover that a higher level of service is required. One of the great quotes I heard in the business is that everyone deserves to be on someone's "A" book. For those new advisors who have not yet reached 100 total client relationships, I would recommend that once you reach 100 clients it becomes an upgrading process, and that if a new client relationship is added, then a smaller, lower-potential client is divested. For those advisors with many more than 100 relationships already, I would recommend that the smaller, less productive, low-potential clients be divested to another advisor who has a smaller minimum and can provide a higher level of service to these smaller relationships.

Once your infrastructure has a manageable number of clients, you need to invest your time and energy in developing a proactive client contact system. In my experience, this proactive monthly client contact should have four parts:

1. Make a connection with the client since the last time you spoke on a personal or professional topic.

2. Conduct a portfolio review. Prepare an update on the client's investment portfolio and how it relates to the current market environment.

3. Use marketing leverage. This is where a good relationship with the client really comes into play. Examples could include client referrals, positioning the contact with other advisors (influencers), suggesting additional, appropriate products and/or services, inviting a client and guest to attend a fun or educational event, or suggesting the client bring in "assets held away."

4. Ask the "anything else" question. End the monthly contact by saying, "Is there anything else on your mind that you would like to bring to my attention?" This facilitates open communication and gives clients a chance to bring up what's on their mind.

The quarterly review should include the same format as the monthly contact, except that it is more formalized and expanded. I recommend that whenever possible, the quarterly reviews be done in person. Another planning session should occur once a year during the annual review. This annual review should be an even more detailed evaluation of the portfolio, as well as the opportunity to modify the client plan and fine-tune and update it as needed. I further recommend that an agenda be used in the annual review, to be organized to cover a lot of material in a reasonable period of time.

An ideal time recommendation for each proactive client contact is as follows:

Type of Review	Time Required
Monthly contact	30 minutes
Quarterly review	45–60 minutes; replace monthly contact
Formal planning session	1 to 1½ hours; replace monthly contact and quarterly review

This schedule translates to approximately 10 hours a year, including client events—quarterly and annual reviews replace those monthly contacts per client—or approximately 50 percent of an advisor's working hours to implement this proactive client contact system.

Focusing on Performance to Achieve Service Excellence

In this instance, I am referring to performance relative to the individual client's goals, and not absolute performance. There are so many factors that are necessary for the proper asset allocation strategy that measuring performance on an absolute basis is not a fair measurement. You must remind clients that they have allocated their assets based on their risk tolerance, and because of the mix of asset classes, their performance might not be the same as a stock market index or compared to a friend who might be taking much more risk to achieve a higher return. The objective is to tie performance back to the overall plan and risk tolerance, not the performance for a given quarter. The index to be measured against should be the "plan index" not the S&P 500. There is no doubt that financial gains are important to client retention, but that performance should always be related to the achievement of the client's long-term objectives. Oftentimes clients need to be reminded of the long-term picture and not be distracted by the short-term volatility that is inherent in the markets. During Bear Market periods when most portfolios are down and performance discussions are most difficult you must be your client's partner—providing continual updates, putting things in a longer term perspective, and helping them keep their emotions from making poor investment decisions.

Expanding Your Service Offerings

The advisor should attempt to be a "one-stop shop" for clients and the "quarterback" for their entire financial situation. However, this relationship may not happen at the beginning. The monthly contact is an excellent time for you to suggest appropriate additional products or services that you can provide that would fit well into the client's overall plan. Examples include:

- Lending opportunities
- Banking services
- Mortgages
- Estate planning
- College funding 529 accounts
- Health savings accounts

❑ Retirement plans

❑ Asset protection (insurance)

The client associate can also recommend different convenience services that might fit well with a client's situation. Examples include:

❑ Online bill payments

❑ Direct deposit

❑ Credit/debit cards

Developing a Plan for Problem Resolution

Not only is problem resolution important, but communication between yourself and the client always needs to be crystal clear. I recommend that ahead of time, you develop a standard operating procedure (SOP) for problem solving.

The SOP should include the steps that each of the team members use when a problem cannot be resolved immediately. Sometimes, the problem simply needs to be brought to someone at a higher level of authority. I've found that in most cases, reasonable problems can be resolved if brought to the attention of the right person. Too often issues get mired down by people who do not have the authority or confidence to solve them themselves. The strategy I've taken is that each advisor must "own" his clients' problems. Some issues that might come up are the timely reporting of tax statements to accountants, delivery of stocks, funds transfers, the transfer of assets or funds to another account, fee reversals, and distributions from retirement accounts—all are examples of business dealings where problems can occur that need a timely resolution. The resolution of any of these problems can be delegated, but the senior advisor must oversee it and take ultimate responsibility for the outcome.

The following is a sample SOP that can serve as a guideline for setting up your own system of client resolution. This system is based on an advisor working with a team for a larger financial services firm. This SOP model is also based on a branch office/regional infrastructure. For advisors working as independents or Registered Investment Advisors, the model needs to be adapted to the support structure that you have. The most important concept is the advisor taking ownership of the problem, overseeing the resolution, communicating to the client, and elevating the problem until a satisfactory resolution is made.

Standard Operating Procedure for Problem Resolution

Step 1: Delegation of Affluent Client's Problem that Needs to Be Resolved—"A" Priority

◻ Client associate attempts to resolve the "A" priority problem within one business day (two days at the latest).

◻ If successful, the client associate communicates the successful resolution to both the client and senior financial advisor.

◻ If the problem cannot be resolved by the client associate within one business day, the senior advisor is immediately notified.

Step 2: Senior Financial Advisor Attempts to Resolve the Client Problem

◻ Senior financial advisor works to resolve the problem during daily administrative time.

◻ If the problem is resolved, the client is immediately notified.

◻ If the problem is not resolved within the next 24 hours, the operations manager or administrative manager is notified.

◻ Client is notified of status of problem and expected next steps.

Step 3: Operations/Administrative Manager
Attempts to Resolve the Client Problem

◻ Operations/administrative manager works to resolve problem.

◻ If the problem is resolved, the senior financial advisor and client are notified.

◻ If the problem is not resolved within one business day, the branch manager is notified.

Step 4: Branch Manager Attempts to
Resolve the Client Problem

◻ Branch manager works to resolve the problem.

◻ When the problem is resolved, the senior financial advisor is notified.

◻ Financial advisor notifies client of problem resolution.

Creating the "New Account" Experience

The initial interactions between an advisor and a client will set the stage for their entire relationship. Having a positive new relationship experience also sets the stage for client referrals. That's why there is never a more important time to provide flawless service than during the first 90 days. Everyone on the team must be committed to doing their part. Standard operating procedures for this event should be set up in advance.

To start, create a new account checklist that everyone on the team follows. This checklist can include all paperwork that needs to be completed and reviewed. Next your client associate should have a proactive introductory call to the client, as well as a follow-up call to review the first statement. The proactive monthly contacts should start immediately. You should check in with clients after the first 90 days and ask how it is going. When the client responds positively, you can take the opportunity to ask, "Is there anyone else that you know that would benefit from the way we do business?"

The Extra Touch

Supplemental contacts can often make the difference in the client's perception of exceptional service. Supplemental contacts are "over and above" the proactive monthly contacts, and they make the affluent client feel important. There are limitless opportunities if you can increase your awareness level and incorporate supplemental contacts into your service model. Here are some examples that I have found to be successful:

- Sending your clients birthday cards with movie ticket gift certificates, or calling to wish them a happy birthday

- Sending a handwritten note on the anniversary of opening the account

- Congratulating clients on their professional accomplishments or personal achievements, including those of family members

- Taking note of personal interests and sending clients related information or inviting them to events they would enjoy

- Having the manager of the office (if applicable) call and thank clients for their business

All of these service extras go back to the top advisors' understanding that as the affluence of the client increases, so does the service requirement. Providing a positive client service experience is one of the most important steps an advisor can take in the journey toward top advisor status.

13

Time Management

OUR TOP ADVISORS recognize the value of their time and how important it is to use their time productively. It's not so much how many hours they put into their business, but how those hours are filled doing the right things. While all of our advisors would consider themselves to be hard workers, they aren't wasting their days with tasks that are not adding to their bottom line.

A Puritanical Work Ethic

The work ethic of many of our top advisors, especially early in their careers, is legendary within our business. For example, Joseph knew from the beginning that he was different from the other advisors he worked with. "I think it was my discipline. I made 175 prospect contacts a week during my first year," he says. "I noticed that the biggest producer in our office was always in at 7:00 a.m., and so I decided that I would get in before him, a habit I still follow. During my first five years, I worked from 6:30 a.m. to 8:00 p.m. every Monday through Thursday. On Friday afternoons, all the guys would go to the bar and I would have six more calls to make, and I always made them. It was during one of the last three or four calls on Friday afternoon that I would often find a prospect."

John shares that he worked at least 80 hours a week during his first two years in the business. In his words, "I knew that I had an incredible opportunity in this career, and I wanted to make sure I succeeded. The only thing I could control in the beginning was how I spent my time. I would not allow the one factor I had absolute control over to be the difference between my success and failure." John's hard work paid off; he reached the million-dollar level by his fifth year in the business, 25 years ago.

Anne credits a big part of her success to her hard work. She explains: "In the beginning, I worked 13 hours a day during the weekdays, and every Saturday and Sunday morning. I was surprised that people didn't work harder in my office, especially in the early part of their careers."

Mike was under pressure to succeed when he started in the business. "When I was hired I was charged with building a significant client base, and the unstated rule of thumb was that I had two years to get to the point where my fees exceeded my salary; otherwise I would be released. I had a strong fear of failure and worked very, very hard," he says. "I lived and breathed this business in the beginning of my career and I did whatever it took. I spent a lot of time traveling, time away from home, a lot of nights and weekends away from things I wanted to be doing. The whole reason I got into the business was so that my success would be a function of what I did, not waiting for somebody to do something for me." Mike provides this advice to aspiring top advisors: "Early on, one needs to realize that they have a limited amount of time, so a sense of urgency is critical." Mike reached $4 million by his seventh year in the business.

Greg was fortunate that he became part of a team early in his career, but that was the result of hard work. He says, "I would always come in early; I would be in the office by 7:00 a.m. There was a very successful senior broker who came in at 7:00, and we were the only ones in the office. He saw my work ethic and offered me a job to work with him as his junior partner. I would work with him all day, reviewing clients' portfolios until dinner, and then we would entertain clients. I was working 24/7 before 24/7 was a term."

A Typical Day

Our top advisors are in a hurry, focused on what they are doing, and always busy. When I worked with them directly, I rarely could just "drop in" because they were always on the phone or had a client in their office. They seldom spent time with other advisors and did not take part in office "gossip" or "politics." If they were not on a lunch appointment, they ate at their desks, because they were too busy to socialize.

Joseph once told me that he is not actually part of the fabric of his office, because he never spends much time with other advisors: "I have never gone to lunch with any of the advisors in the office. I would just get something to eat at my desk, which is what I do to this day." Joseph gets to work between 6:00 and 6:30 a.m. and works until 4:30 p.m. During the middle of the day he goes to work out for an hour. During the summer, he leaves early one day a week to play golf, leaving work at noon. He estimates that 90 percent of his time is spent with clients and prospects.

Ross has a similar outlook and schedule. "When I'm on the job, I'm not going to socialize with the guys. I am there for a purpose, and that is to do the best possible job for our clients and team. I rarely go out to lunch. In fact, most of the time my team eats at their desk." Ross starts his day reading *The Wall Street Journal*, checking e-mail, and developing his business ideas. Then he determines what money came due and looks at his scheduled calls. "I usually have three to four scheduled calls or reviews every day, plus two client or prospect meetings," he says. "We encourage clients to come to our office: That's where the tools of our trade are. We have lunch at 11:30 and leave between four and six." Ross estimates that 65 percent of his time is spent interacting with clients and prospects. He spends on average an hour a day making marketing contacts, prospect follow-up calls, or prospect appointments.

I recently caught up with Sam after not seeing him for five years. While we had a great relationship when I was his manager, we had lost touch. When we met, Sam apologized for the lack of contact, but admitted, "It's not that I don't care about you, it's honestly that I have very little emotional energy left after spending time focusing on the relationships that are important to my business, and what energy I have left over is reserved for my family." No offense taken, Sam. He describes himself as very regimented and predictable, saying, "I work out at the same times every day. I go to bed at the same time every night. I wake up early. I don't waste time. I go hard all day from 7:30 a.m. to 5:30 p.m. I start the day catching up on e-mails, reading the news, and getting a sense of what's going on for the day. I start preparing for meetings, reviews, portfolio analysis, meeting with my team. Then, about nine the phone starts ringing. I spend the rest of the day doing client reviews, getting calls, and making proactive calls." Sam estimates that at least 50 percent of his time is spent with clients and another 10 percent on marketing activities, which he regrets. "I'm not prospecting enough," he says. "That's the single biggest weakness that I have. I enjoy prospecting, but I'm not doing it the way I use to."

Anne usually works at home in the mornings from 6:00 a.m. to 9:00 a.m., going through e-mails, making calls, and checking to make sure nothing has fallen through the cracks. She gets to the office by 10:00 a.m. and stays until 4:00 p.m. three days a week. Two days she works at night, usually entertaining clients or prospects. She also tries to work at least one morning on the weekends, doing administrative-related work. Anne estimates that she spends 70 percent of her working day with clients and prospects and 30 percent with her team on administrative issues, reviews of proposals, and follow-up activities. Of the 70 percent of her time devoted to clients and prospects, 20 percent is spent on the prospecting side.

William uses the following analogy: "If you come in at eight and punch out at five, then you are a renter. If you believe that your time is your own, you'll work extra hard Monday through Thursday so that you can play golf on Friday, then you're an owner. I have guys in the office that tell me I act like I own the place, and I thought that was the best compliment I'd ever received. Because it's not an ego issue; it's the fact that I feel like an owner not a renter." William describes his typical schedule as starting every day at 8:30 a.m. and working until 5:30 p.m. on Mondays and Wednesdays, and till 3:30 p.m. on the other days, and then he takes as many Fridays off as he can. When asked how much time he spent prospecting, he answers, "One hundred percent of my waking hours I'm thinking about marketing—whether I'm with my clients, [at my] church group, on an airplane, playing golf, it's always on my mind. I'm always looking for the right opportunities to build relationships that could lead to business."

John starts his day by working out at 6:00 a.m. (at his home). He has breakfast with his kids and gets to work by 8:15 a.m. At nine he has a conference call scheduled with a client or prospect, another one at ten and one at eleven. He typically goes to lunch with a client at 11:30 a.m. and gets back by 1:00 p.m. He has conference calls scheduled at one and two in the afternoon with a prospect or client. John explains that "usually every hour, on the hour, there is something scheduled for me to do. My team keeps me booked throughout the day. For example, today I had eight meetings, and of those, two were in person, and the rest were conference calls. Four of those calls were with prospects we were working with." John estimates he spends 70 percent of his time with prospects and clients; the majority of it is working to get new clients. He tries to leave at 5:30 p.m., except Monday night, when he works late. He also travels on average three days a month. John believes in working hard and playing hard, and after 30 years in the business, he spends his weekends with his family and takes six weeks off a year on personal vacations.

Rob divides his day in thirds. As he explains, "I'm looking for a third of my time in business development, a third of my time on investment strategy, and a third of my time on client reviews. Business development is my responsibility for the team; my partner does all the implementation of our business."

Jack is among the hardest working of our top advisors. He has been in the business for more than 40 years and still gets to the office at 8:30 a.m., after he has exercised in the morning, then he works until 5:30 p.m. to 6:00 p.m. most nights. He explains that he only goes out to lunch a few times a year, because lunch is a good time for his clients to reach him.

Even though our top advisors all work hard and focus on the right activities, they also make time for their families and personal time. Even though the hours are long, these advisors enjoy what they do, interacting with clients professionally and personally, as well as the thrill of growing their practices through business development. Jack speaks for many of the top advisors when he says, "I don't think of it in terms of whether I'm working or not working, it's just who I am."

Implementing Lesson #13

All the top advisors continue to work hard, but not the way they did when they first started out. As they built their successful practices, they began to work smarter as they learned from experience effective time-management techniques. For example, this business has been and always will be about building relationships with affluent investors. Our top advisors understood early in their careers that to be successful, they needed to spend most of their time getting in front of people who had money, and then cultivating those relationships in order to build trust. There were no shortcuts to the process of building relationships, and that's where the majority of their time continues to be spent. Some of our advisors are more structured with their time than others, but they all have a common focus on the activities that counted—prospect and client relationships.

I asked every top advisor what percentage of their day was spent with clients and prospects. The range was from 50 percent to 90 percent of their working hours. That includes hours spent in the office, as well as time spent in nonprofit leadership activities, engagements entertaining clients, and other outside activities that involve clients and prospects.

The Importance of Delegating

For the most part, our top advisors are able to delegate administrative activities to their team members; in fact, they built their teams around the idea that having top-notch support staff would enable them to spend more time with prospects and clients. As William says, "Too many advisors do not put a price on their time, but when you're making photocopies, you're making $8 an hour; when you are doing a client review, you're making $500 an hour."

Mike describes his view on delegation as follows: "As I progressed in my career I learned to delegate. Early in my career, being a control freak, I wanted to own everything, to make sure it was done right. Now I've gotten to a point where I recognize that I need to own the really important things, but that I can't possibly own everything. So I delegate much more of the administrative aspects of clients needs."

Anne told me that she is a great delegator. "My practice is like an assembly line," she says. "I delegate as much as I possibly can to the rest of my team or I would have no quality of life. I am also the kind of person who overstaffs, and I have been willing to pay more so that I could have the team capacity to delegate."

The only way for you to spend more time with clients and prospects is to delegate as much of the nonrelationship activities as possible to someone else. The first step is to determine what can be delegated and to whom. Those tasks that can be delegated should be prioritized and assigned with a deadline. An example might be "A" tasks done in one business day, "B" tasks done within one week, and "C" tasks completed whenever there is time.

A meeting should occur every day between the advisor and team member responsible for completion of the delegated tasks. At the meeting, the advisor hands over the task to be completed along with its priority ranking, and the team member hands back the tasks that have already been completed. The advisor checks the tasks off against a list of delegated tasks. The team member lets the advisor know if any client-related problem resolution issues are delayed, according to the client resolution "SOP," or standard operating procedure (as covered in Chapter 12). This daily meeting should last between 15 to 30 minutes.

Time Blocking

Our top advisors group similar activities together, as opposed to doing all sorts of different type of activities within an hour. This is a process called *time blocking*. They might do the monthly client contacts or reviews during one part of the day, and marketing contacts and appointments at another time. For example, Ross schedules his week ahead of time to make the most of time blocking. He does all of his client contacts and appointments on Monday, Tuesday, and Wednesday. On Thursday and Friday, he leaves a slot of the schedule for marketing and prospecting activities.

There is a rhythm and efficiency that occurs when similar tasks are done together; tasks get easier as momentum is built and you get better at doing them. It takes discipline not to get distracted during a time block, but the payoff is worth it in terms of productivity.

Prioritization

How you spend your time will define your success. One of the most important lessons we can learn from our top advisors is how they make use of time. They all spend the majority of their day focused on clients and affluent prospect contacts and appointments.

One of the best time-management tools to help with prioritization is a time log. This is an invaluable tool for you to see how actual time is spent versus perceived time. It can also serve as a firm motivator to adjust your schedule and behavior to align your time spent with the schedules of our top advisors.

I recommend using a time log for at least one month, but it can certainly be used for a longer time period. The idea is to keep track of how you spend your time during the day, working in 30-minute increments. As you go through your log, you should record how each 30 minutes was spent, labeled by activity. Activity categories could include:

- ◻ Client contact

- ◻ Prospect contact

- ◻ Administration

- ◻ Team meetings

- ◻ Office meetings

- ◻ Preparation

- ◻ Reading

❑ Training

❑ Other

After a few days, you will see how you are literally spending your day. Client and prospect contact time (calls and appointments) should be divided into total working time to determine the percentage of productive time spent every day. If the daily and cumulative number is less than 50 percent, then your schedule should be adjusted to make sure more than 50 percent of your time is productive.

The Schedule

Developing a schedule that is followed every day helps put the necessary daily activities into a workable framework. No day is perfect, and the daily schedule should be viewed as a guideline, not an absolute. As in any business, too many "surprises" happen each day that make it impossible to follow a schedule perfectly.

I have outlined a sample daily schedule that I have coached advisors to use for years. It is designed to be simple enough to allow flexibility, but structured enough to incorporate the fundamental time-management principles. The schedule is designed for experienced advisors with an established client base, but it can be easily adapted for new advisors simply by substituting the client contact with marketing contacts for appointments with new prospects.

The concept behind this scheduling technique is that up until and during lunch, you are engaged in proactive activities, namely, client contact and bringing in new business. After lunch you move into a reactive mode, which means handling issues from existing clients and other administrative items. This ensures that at least 50 percent of your day is proactive and spent on your priority activities.

To structure your day this way, the schedule places the most important and most proactive activities earliest in the day: client and prospective client contact. By scheduling the highest-priority activities first, you will ensure that they are likely to be accomplished. Lunch is an ideal time for a prospect or client appointment and follows the time-management principles employed by our top advisors, all of whom use the lunch hour effectively. All other activities that are not related to client and prospect contacts and appointments should be done in the afternoon. Being "available but not on call" in the morning is the operative concept. This means you will be available to return nonmarket-related calls in the afternoon after the proactive part of your day is completed.

Clients will accept getting called back within a reasonable period of time (within the day), unless it is an important market action item. E-mail can be a huge distraction and should be postponed until the afternoon. The afternoons can certainly be used for additional client and prospect contact and appointments, but this time should be flexible to accommodate the necessary administrative requirements of the job.

Sample Schedule

8:00–10:30:   Monthly client contact, quarterly and annual reviews

10:30–12:00:   Prospect pipeline contact, marketing contacts for new prospect appointments

12:00–1:30:   Lunch/Client or Prospect appointment

1:30–5:00:   Returning phone calls, e-mails, and other administrative duties

Creating Repeatable Processes

Every aspect of this business is process-based, which means that there is a process in place for every important function of the job. By creating the right processes for your business, you are ensuring that you will experience a minimal level of downtime during the day so that you will be able to spend at least 50 percent of your time on the highest-priority activities. For example, most client reviews and marketing presentations can be created in advance based on a template that can be customized in minutes. Your investment strategy can easily be executed by your team once that template is set.

In John's words, "We really try to have procedures that are very repeatable. We have an e-mail prepared in advance for prospects that talks about our team and our experience and approach to the business. And you really have to make sure that tasks are properly assigned. If I have quarterly reviews coming up, my staff automatically knows what needs to be done. I will review their work to check and make sure it is right, but they know what each review is going to look like for the quarter because it has been mass-produced."

Like John, William believes strongly in having established processes in his practice. "I'm very much of a systems guy," William says. "I write to my team in blue ink, they write to me in black, and we do corrections in red. Our processes are set up so that we are systematically touching our clients. We send birthday cards, Thanksgiving cards, and small holiday gifts. If we need to make an investment change, we'll pull a cross-post and then a registered member of my team will make the calls to clients to recommend the change. That gives people confidence that we're watching the accounts between reviews."

You can develop established processes for the following activities:

◻ *Monthly Client Contact/Quarterly Reviews.* You need a process that tracks which clients have been contacted each month, and which clients need to be contacted. Information needs to be available on each client regarding the client's investment performance, product/service expansion, and assets held away, which necessitates taking notes, and the ability to access notes taken, during the last contact. Quarterly reviews and annual reviews should have agendas prepared in advance and sent to clients before reviews are held.

◻ *Prospect's First Appointment.* Questions should be prepared in advance to ask prospects about their current investment situation

◻ *Prospect Presentation.* The presentation—called a pitch book—should provide information about the firm, the team, the wealth-management process, resources, and recommended next steps. It should be high quality, condensed, and practiced. The purpose of the pitch book is to be used during the second appointment, to share with the prospects what they could expect from you as their advisor.

◻ *Prospect Pipeline Management.* A contact system can be established so that each prospect is contacted at least once a month. Notes can be taken and referred to, and a checklist of relationship-building activities can be referred to during the prospecting process.

◻ *New Account Checklist.* A checklist should be developed and followed by the responsible team member to ensure a quality new account experience. See Chapter 12 for more details.

◻ *Call Screening.* Develop a process for how you would like the phone to be answered by the team. The client associate should offer to help; if the offer is not accepted, then he should say when the advisor will call back.

◻ *Problem Resolution.* Establish a standard operating procedure for all team members to use in the resolution of client problems. See Chapter 12 for more details.

◻ *Wealth-Management Process.* This process should include planning questions, development of an investment plan and asset allocation strategy, plan presentation, and follow up. See Chapter 11 for more details.

◻ *Investment Process.* For this activity, you need a process for identifying what investment vehicles are to be used to implement the investment portion of the wealth-management process.

PART TWO: PUTTING THE LESSONS INTO PRACTICE

14

Taylor Glover: Lessons from the Very Top

ONE OF OUR top financial advisors stood out from the rest, in my opinion, as the "very top" of the group and the industry. His name is Taylor Glover, and he worked at a large, national financial services firm in Atlanta. Taylor retired from that firm after 30 years and is currently the president and CEO of Turner Enterprises. The lessons that can be learned from Taylor are so powerful and important that I felt that it was worthwhile to have a single chapter focused on him and his business practices.

I worked with Taylor for four years when I was the manager of the Atlanta office at this national financial services firm, and I learned as much about our business from observing him as any experience in my career. Taylor was the number-one financial advisor at his firm during the four years that I was his manager: He had assets under management of $4 billion and generated between $10 million and $15 million in business each year. Watching Taylor at work in many ways was like being the manager of Babe Ruth's Yankees and watching the Babe play baseball firsthand. I recognized that I was witnessing "greatness," and I took full advantage of my position to learn as much as I could from him.

What makes Taylor's story so compelling is that he started in financial services as a 22-year-old college graduate with no connections to the industry at all. Taylor's experience proves that it doesn't require past connections, an MBA, or being part of a big team to be successful. His story shows how powerful many of the success principles and lessons are when executed at the highest level and the enormous amounts of business that will result.

Taylor built his career from the most humble of beginnings and should serve as an inspiration for all financial advisors that aspire to a multimillion-dollar practice. Not everyone can be Taylor Glover, but anyone who is willing to work hard can learn the lessons from the "very top" and, in implementing those lessons, take their practice to a significantly higher level.

In the Beginning . . .

In 1973, Taylor graduated from the University of Georgia and, at age 22, applied at a large, national financial services firm six days later. His decision to work at this firm was based on the urgings of his former roommate, the only person his age he knew working as a financial advisor at the time. This friend introduced Taylor to his manager. During the initial interview the manager asked Taylor if he knew anyone that could invest with him. Taylor responded that he knew 20 people that had at least a $1,000 to invest. (Later, he admitted to me that when he began work, he had absolutely no idea how he was going to build his business). In the end, the manager agreed to send Taylor to New York for an interview, but at Taylor's expense. Taylor had never been on an airplane before and had to borrow money from his brother to pay for the airfare. He got a job offer from the firm after the New York interview.

Taylor worked extremely hard throughout his entire career, but particularly in the beginning. He would get to work at 6:00 a.m. each weekday and worked until 8:00 p.m., and he also worked every Saturday morning. As important as the hours he worked, he also worked smart. Taylor spent his time at work trying to get in front of prospects. He made a decision early in his career that he would not go to lunch with other financial advisors. They were not going to do business with him, so he didn't want to waste his valuable prospecting time. Instead of having lunch with other advisors, he spent that time prospecting. He would often stop into a successful restaurant for lunch and over time he developed a relationship with the owner; eventually, the owner opened an account and become a very significant client.

Taylor didn't know anyone with significant money in Atlanta, so he would go through newspapers and find articles or announcements about good things happening to people or opportunities that showed potential money in motion. He recruited his wife Shearon to write the names of these prospects on index cards to help organize his efforts. Taylor would then cold-call these people and congratulate them, introducing himself and asking for an appointment. He would say, "I know you are familiar with Cobb County [as an example] and they are offering some tax-free bonds. Would you be interested?" If they were interested, he sold them the bonds; if not, he kept them in a follow-up file to call at a later time. In either case he attempted to schedule a face-to-face meeting so that he could meet his prospective clients.

Developing relationships with affluent people was a high priority with Taylor from the get-go. When prospects showed any sign of potential interest, he would keep calling them every month. Every day he had a pile of index cards to work with: some new and some existing prospects. This was the prospecting method that Taylor used to open his first 100 relationships: Many were small accounts, but importantly, some of these small accounts belonged to some affluent individuals who later become very large accounts.

The Next Step: Involvement in Nonprofit Organizations

After acquiring his first 100 clients, Taylor made a pivotal decision to change his marketing methods. In his words, he began to "refine" his approach. Taylor knew that he was good at recognizing potential business opportunities. However, he also knew that he had to be in the right place at the right time in order to meet the level of investor he wanted to pursue. He started to become involved in organizations that had members that he wanted to meet.

Taylor was limited in the beginning by the organizations he could afford to join, but he joined a lot of them. He became a member and a leader in the Kiwanis Club, his college alumni organization, his church group, Ducks Unlimited, and The Quarterback Club. None of these organizations cost a lot of money, but as he began to meet more and more qualified investors, and as his success grew, so did his budget.

Taylor went on in his career to become a member of the most significant boards in Atlanta. He simply kept raising the ante, becoming a leader in the most visible and prestigious nonprofit boards as his career progressed. He became the face of his large, national financial services firm in Atlanta. He had a very strong personal interest in every nonprofit organization he joined, and he always took a leadership position. He impressed the other board members with his energy, commitment, and enthusiasm. Taylor never waited for his firm to contribute to an organization he wanted to be part of. Instead, he financed his memberships himself. In his view, it was a cost of doing business.

As the price of admission increased, so did the wealth of the individuals he was exposed to. He was very careful to approach these opportunities at the appropriate time; he was very cognizant of not coming across too strong, too early. He recognized that the first step was to build a relationship and not to rush the business before the relationship was built.

By 1985, Taylor had many relationships with more than $1 million in assets. He never stopped raising the bar, recognizing that the leverage in this business is the size of the relationship. Taylor acquired several of the $100 million relationships he developed, including a billionaire, from his involvement in various organizations. Sometimes it took more than ten years for these personal relationships to develop into significant business relationships. One of his favorite techniques for transitioning from a personal relationship to a business one was to engage the prospect in a discussion about the market. Whenever he engaged a peer about the stock market, Taylor would turn the question over to the prospect. Taylor would always ask, "I'm looking for ideas right now, what do you like?" This would lead to a conversation about investments. Taylor's objective was to get the prospect into a conversation, find out as much as he could about the person's situation, develop a personal relationship, and over time turn that relationship into a business client.

Taylor Glover Meets Ted Turner

Taylor had a breakthrough when as a young financial advisor he developed a relationship with future billionaire Ted Turner. Taylor met Ted Turner the same way that many people meet Ted, by asking him for money. At the time, Taylor was in a leadership position with Ducks Unlimited and was in charge of their charity auction. Taylor called Ted (a fellow member of DU) and asked him to donate a pair of season tickets to the Atlanta Hawks, the professional basketball team that Turner owned. Ted balked at donating season tickets and offered to donate tickets to a single game. Taylor finally convinced him to donate the season tickets and be his guest at the auction event, which Ted accepted.

During the event, a weekend at a hunting lodge was auctioned as well. Ted got so excited about the event that he offered to donate a weekend at his lodge, and he got a great price for it on behalf of Ducks Unlimited. In the meantime, Ted bought many of the auction items, including live hunting dogs. He asked Taylor if he could take care of his purchases and deliver them to him. Taylor agreed, and the next day he showed up with all the items Ted bought, including the dogs. Ted invited Taylor to join him that next weekend at his hunting lodge to get it ready for the hunters who had purchased a weekend stay at the auction, and once again, Taylor agreed. That was the beginning of a very strong relationship that has lasted for more than 30 years.

However, Taylor didn't start doing real business with Ted Turner until ten years after they met. The millionaire had most of his money tied up in his different and growing businesses, including the Atlanta Braves, the Atlanta Hawks, and CNN. In fact, according to Taylor, "When Ted sold his original billboard company, he invested the money from the sale with me for a year, and then reinvested in his new businesses."

But the fact that Ted didn't do business with Taylor didn't mean he didn't help him indirectly. Ted Turner was a rising star in Atlanta, and being seen as a business associate and friend of Ted Turner's helped facilitate Taylor's reputation as a leader in the community. According to Taylor, "Even though Ted didn't do significant business with me at first, I certainly benefited. People would see us together and assume that Ted invested a lot of money with me. This gave me great credibility with many affluent investors in Atlanta."

Taylor never took advantage of the relationship, and never asked Ted for anything. Taylor paid his own way for everything. He was introduced to Ted's friends, also very wealthy individuals that Taylor would not have had access to otherwise. In many cases, these friends of Ted Turner became clients, and Taylor began to develop a client base of Atlanta's wealthiest individuals.

The $100 Million Club

While I was the manager of the Atlanta office, I asked Taylor if he had a minimum size client relationship, and he responded: "Yes, $100 million." I was astonished. I had known few advisors with a $100 million relationship, never imagining that could be a minimum size for any advisor to work with. To be clear, Taylor's team did work with many relationships under $100 million, but that was the minimum size required for Taylor to work with the client directly. Taylor had acquired at least ten $100 million relationships.

However, Taylor would not have been able to maintain any of these relationships without a strong sense of the "leverage of size" principle, as well as the right mindset. Taylor was never intimidated by or in awe of his largest clients, some of whom were billionaires. Taylor would argue with and challenge his top clients the same as he would a family member or friend. In having the confidence to be himself, Taylor emerges as a peer and friend of his wealthiest clients. Taylor discovered that wealthy individuals would prefer to work with a peer rather than a subordinate.

Many advisors are intimidated by the wealthy and don't show the confidence to attract and retain these individuals as clients. Learn from Taylor's confident approach as he dealt with some of the wealthiest individuals in the country.

Long-Term Orientation

Taylor had a strict prospecting rule: He would never let a big one go, and most of the time he eventually got them as a client. That philosophy epitomizes the long-term orientation success principle. Taylor met the majority of his most affluent clients through outside interests.

For example, Taylor met Brandon through his involvement in Ducks Unlimited. Because of Taylor's leadership position within

DU, he was invited to be a guest, along with other leaders, at Brandon's private hunting club. This was early in Taylor's career, and he saw this invitation as a wonderful opportunity to start a potential business relationship with Brandon. Taylor knew Brandon came from a very wealthy family, so he approached Brandon on this trip and told him that his firm had a very good analyst that covered the industry that Brandon's family business was in, and he offered to provide him with all the current research that his firm had available regarding that industry and to arrange a conference call with the firm's analyst that covered Brandon's company. Brandon responded to Taylor very directly by saying, "I brought you here to hunt, not to talk business. I have people that read all these reports and provide me reports on the reports, and I have no interest in getting research from your firm."

Taylor was embarrassed. There was no escape from the hunting trip since the transportation to get there had been provided, so Taylor just sulked and removed himself from the group. That afternoon Brandon approached Taylor and offered to take him in his canoe to hunt. Taylor agreed, and that's when a relationship began to develop.

For years, the relationship continued, but no mention of business was made by either Brandon or Taylor. Brandon was sent around the country to learn the family business. Taylor stayed in touch, mostly through Christmas cards and an occasional call or visit when Brandon came home to Atlanta. Eight years later, Brandon returned to Atlanta permanently and invited Taylor to hunt with him. On the ride back, he told Taylor, "I'm getting a small trust distribution and wanted to know if you would manage it for me?" Taylor did a good job of managing the trust for him, and Brandon referred him to his aunt, the matriarch of the family business. Over time, these two relationships both had in excess of $100 million in assets with Taylor.

Another important part of his long-term orientation was his willingness to spend his own money as an investment in the growth of his business. Taylor was a believer in "retained earnings," and as the wealth of his clients and prospects grew, so did the amount of money that he spent. He made personal donations to be on the most prestigious boards in Atlanta. He purchased a jet, hired a pilot, and paid all his fuel expenses because that was the most efficient way for him to travel (and private air travel is the way his clients and friends traveled). He never let any of these costs get in the way of a good business investment. Taylor's expenses might seem extreme, but they didn't start that way. Yet as his business success grew, so did his expenditures. As he made money in the business he was always willing to reinvest it back into his business.

Specialization

As Taylor began to accumulate wealth himself, he developed an interest and expertise in investing in private and start-up companies. Taylor learned how successful businesses were built, and developed an expertise in working with successful entrepreneurs. For example, in the late-1990s, a young entrepreneur approached Taylor about providing funding for a small company he wanted to bring public. The entrepreneur had been referred through Taylor's cousin, and he was looking for potential investors. The young entrepreneur had recently graduated from college, and after meeting him, Taylor liked his business idea and provided a portion of the investment capital needed. The company was sold within six months for two and a half times his initial investment. Taylor took the money and the gains that he made on the first venture and invested it with the same entrepreneur to fund another innovative idea, which eventually became a well-known publicly traded company. As a result, this man became part of Taylor's $100 million clients from the proceeds of the sale of his company.

Relationship Building

Taylor, perhaps the greatest relationship builder I had ever worked with, told me that his most significant client relationships started as friendships. Taylor describes his best clients as his three closest friends. He describes his relationships as follows: "If I called any one of these three right now, no matter where in the world they are, they will answer my call. I have a relationship with each one of their assistants that is as tight as the one I have with my own assistant."

Another one of Taylor's clients was the CEO of a very well known Fortune 500 company. Taylor met Rick (not his real name) through his wife, Shearon, who played tennis with Rick's wife. As a couple, they began to build a relationship with Rick and his wife. Initially, Rick was skeptical of Taylor because of his position as a financial advisor. Over the years, as their relationship grew and they became friends, Rick felt comfortable talking to Taylor about financial and investment matters.

When Taylor encouraged Rick to consider establishing an investment banking relationship with his firm, Rick was interested. Up to that point Rick had used another large firm, but Taylor made a case that the power of his firm's retail distribution was a real asset. Rick agreed, and Taylor made the introduction to the investment bankers. A big deal was consummated and Taylor got a significant referral fee. When Rick later departed from the company, he sought Taylor for advice in negotiating a settlement. And Taylor, through several referrals to attorneys, helped Rick negotiate a very favorable settlement.

Taylor once met one of Atlanta's most prominent and successful citizens, whom we'll call Cameron, at an exclusive golf course in Atlanta. Taylor had been sponsored to this golf club by another affluent client. Cameron would frequently ask Taylor about investments and the markets, and while Taylor never solicited his business, he would provide Cameron with his best ideas. On one occasion Cameron asked Taylor about an investment banking underwriting for his company, and Taylor introduced Cameron to the investment bankers that covered his industry. The investment bankers were impressed with Cameron's company and the deal was completed. This was just the beginning of their business relationship. Today,

Taylor is currently on the board of directors of Cameron's company, and Cameron had over $100 million in assets invested with Taylor.

When I arrived in Atlanta as the manager in 1998, I witnessed a phenomenon I had never seen before. Taylor was providing his firm's investment bankers with access to the companies they were attempting to do business with. When the investment bankers would call on some of the top Atlanta companies, they were told by the CEOs to go through Taylor first, because he was their relationship at the firm. I have never seen as many humble investment bankers as I did when I was in Atlanta. If they wanted access they had to go through Taylor, and if a deal was done with one of Taylor's clients, he got an investment banking referral fee.

Service

When Taylor was asked what he thought was the difference between himself and other advisors, his answer was that he had been "road tested" early in his career from some of the most interesting but demanding clients, like Ted Turner, who had a lot of money but also very high expectations. As Taylor's circle of clients and friends grew in affluence, so did their expectations, and in all cases he rose to the occasion. In fact, he felt his greatest value to his clients was not his investment strategy, although he did that well, but the family-office-type service he gave to his clients.

Wealth Management

While Taylor enjoyed investing for clients, his highest priority was always the relationship. He spent much more time helping his clients with noninvestment needs than their actual investments. He acted as a family office for his wealthiest clients, and as a result, they did their investment business with him. This is typical of the wealth-management business model.

· His investment philosophy overall was conservative. Taylor built large positions with high-quality companies, many of which were local.

His favorite companies were near-monopolies that had high barriers of entry. He would buy and hold and typically just sell the losing positions. He had a low turnover portfolio and in most cases a discretionary investment relationship with his best clients. He had primarily a value approach to investments. His philosophy was that not selling was sometimes the best investment management he could provide.

Taylor and his team did the investment management themselves, as he felt most of his largest clients wanted him to be the money manager. He eventually delegated the investment side of the business to his team members, who understood and followed his investment philosophy and guidelines. Because of his family office approach, Taylor was the quarterback for his best clients' entire financial needs, going beyond just their investments.

The Team

When I became the manager of the Atlanta office in 1998, Taylor had developed a world-class team. Yet it took him 25 years of team building before he ended up with his "A Team" that supported and enabled him to achieve a $15 million practice. Taylor recognized early in his career that the more he was able to interact with wealthy individuals, the more successful he would be. He built his team to enable him to do just that.

The first person on his team was his wife, Shearon. Shearon helped him find and organize his prospect leads and supported him on any other tasks that he needed help with. Soon after, Taylor shared an assistant with four other advisors, but as his business grew he eventually got the one-on-one support he needed.

Within a few years of reaching $1 million and having his own assistant, Taylor met and hired Ruthie Bolvig as his primary assistant. Twenty-plus years later, Ruthie is still Taylor's primary assistant. She was exactly what he needed. Her pivotal role was enabling him to get out of the office. No matter where Taylor was, she covered for him, handled what she could, and made sure that he got back to whomever he needed to call back. Everything is filtered through Ruthie before it goes to Taylor.

The next key member of the team was Art, who Taylor got to know through his involvement with Buckhead Bank in 1991. Art was one of the senior bankers who particularly impressed Taylor, and when Art showed some interest in working together, Taylor quickly offered him a job. Art was making about $75K at the bank, and Taylor offered him $60K and a bonus, depending on how well the team did. Art accepted the job, and within the first two years he was making more than $400K.

Taylor felt his time was best spent with his best clients, but as he was building his team he knew he needed to set up the investment process and manage the personnel issues. He didn't enjoy the personnel aspect of the business and eventually Art took over those roles. Art also worked with those relationships that were not part of Taylor's largest relationships but which he had acquired over his many years in the business. Art would review all the phone messages and handle as many clients as he could himself; he managed Taylor's calendar and provided him with talking points for meetings. Art also became a "scribe" for Taylor. As Taylor met with his larger relationships, Art would accompany him and take notes, then make sure all the follow-up steps were taken and promises delivered upon. Art evolved into the chief operating officer for the team.

The next key member of the team was Austin, who had impressed Taylor as an intern in 1996. Austin replaced Art as Taylor's scribe for his largest relationships and would accompany Taylor on his meetings, taking notes on what follow-up was needed and ensuring that it would get done. Taylor wanted his largest relationships to be comfortable working with Art and Austin, so he positioned them as his partners, which facilitated the relationship-building process between them and his best clients.

Taylor would assign Art or Austin as a backup on his client relationships. Whenever the client needed something, Taylor would involve Art or Austin. In that way clients would know that it was Art or Austin who got things done, and before long they would just bypass Taylor and go right to one of the other men. Taylor, meanwhile, was always available as needed, whether for quarterly reviews or for sticking his head into a meeting.

The team eventually developed a formal client stratification model:

Platinum   10 to 20 key relationships, $100 million + (Taylor)

Gold   Next 40 clients (Art and Austin)

Silver   Clients 50 to 200 (Art and Austin)

Bronze   All other accounts, minimum size $2,500 in business (assigned to registered administrative assistants)

Every time I was in Taylor's office, he was talking to his clients, and it was seldom about their investments. Instead, it was about what was going on in their lives. From my observations, Taylor spent 100 percent of his time on the relationship aspect of the business. He had already set in motion the investment process, and his team was busy executing it. That left him plenty of time to build relationships.

The team was vertically organized around supporting Taylor. Once a year the team would meet offsite and go through each client relationship and strategize about how to elevate each relationship. Taylor had a seven-figure payroll for his team, beyond the salaries that his firm was paying them.

Taylor, According to Art

Art Rollins worked side by side with Taylor for more than 12 years and had as good a perspective on Taylor's qualities as anyone. According to Art, Taylor had six essential qualities:

1. He was a "time miser," a no-nonsense professional, spending his time on the right things.

2. He was able to communicate complicated concepts in an easy-to-understand way.

3. He was the quintessential networker.

4. He was not intimidated by big money.

5. His focus was on developing relationships.

6. He had an intense focus on goals and achieving them.

Of all those qualities, Taylor's ability to network and connect with people was his most powerful. He had four passions: his family, church, hunting, and philanthropy. He centered his networking and marketing skills on those passions, and in many ways his business and personal life were interwoven. Taylor was able to open the door to business relationships through his disarming passion for their mutual interests. He was very patient in turning personal relationships into business relationships, but was very successful at making that transition.

Taylor was both competitive and goal-oriented. When Taylor worked with me, the only score sheet he was interested in was his national ranking within the firm. He always wanted to make sure he was number one, and he was interested to know who his competitors were. It was a healthy competition that provided the energy required to work as hard as he did. This competitive sprit never compromised his integrity, because Taylor was among the most ethical advisors that I worked with.

Marketing

Taylor marketed through his passions: hunting and philanthropy. His approach was coming into a room and holding court—providing humor, telling stories, making personal connections quickly by connecting to things that he and his clients had in common. Taylor was always entertaining prospects and clients, developing these relationships through sporting events, hunting trips, and entertaining with his wife. He used his involvement in philanthropic organizations to meet affluent prospects, establish mutual interests, and develop those relationships. According to Art, there were only one or two occasions when Taylor didn't convert a personal relationship into a significant business relationship.

By 1991, Taylor had really started to leverage his relationship with Ted Turner and became an insider in the media communications industry in Atlanta. He earned his way into the inner circles of the super affluent communications players. He changed his business structure and started to focus on becoming a *family office* to ten key relationships. The family-office approach meant advising clients in all facets of their life, not just their investments. He had transcended from a financial advisor to an indispensable partner. For example, Taylor helped Ted Turner organize his many and significant charitable contributions, his antinuclear efforts, and his vast land holdings. He had the same type of relationship with most of his significant relationships.

With his team in place, Taylor could turn his efforts to building relationships with some of the wealthiest individuals in the country. He was out of the city more often, and out of the office more than in it. Taylor was meeting with the likes of Bill Clinton and Bill Gates through Ted Turner. He purchased a jet and hired a pilot to accommodate his need to travel to entertain his prospects and clients, as well as provide his brand of family-office services.

Taylor's business grew exponentially during this time, validating his business model. In 1991, Taylor did $1.8 million in business; in 2000, he did $15 million.

Time Management

Art describes Taylor as a "time miser." Taylor never spent time with anyone in the office other than his team. The only time any of the other advisors in the office saw him was when he came in or left. The other advisors in the office inferred that he was a ghost, because he came in quietly and spent 100 percent of his office time on the phone talking to his clients and prospects. I worked with Taylor in the same building for those four years and he didn't know where my office was located. It wasn't that we didn't communicate; it was just that I always visited him in his office. Although he would pick up the phone and call me, Taylor had too much going on to visit my office.

Some of our coworkers considered him to be antisocial, but the truth is that he was just the opposite: He was extremely social, but spent that energy with his clients and prospects, not the other advisors. This was how he was able to stay true to what was important to him: His priorities were his business and his family, and he didn't waste time doing anything else.

Professional Growth

Taylor's professional growth came more from his own experience of seeing how successful businesses were built and run, rather than from achieving a professional designation. He was involved in many outside investment interests throughout his career; as a result, he received a real-world education on how successful businesses were built. He would share this understanding and experience with many of his successful clients and frequently acted as an advisor on business decisions that they made. His value to them went beyond the investments he recommended, and extended to his advice on how they could run their business better and more effectively. He transcended the role of financial advisor and became an "unofficial" partner to a number of his clients.

Professional Referral Sources

As Taylor's reputation in Atlanta grew as one of the most prominent and visible financial advisors in the community, he had no shortage of other professionals willing to provide referrals to him. In his case, becoming a "pillar of the community" and working with many of

Atlanta's most prominent citizens gave him great leverage, providing the reputation and credibility for other professionals to refer their clients to him. Most often he would develop relationships with potential referral sources by meeting them the same way he met his best clients—through mutual friends and involvement in nonprofit organizations. In Taylor's case, this was an indirect or secondary marketing strategy rather than a primary one.

The Personal Side

I was sharing some of the lessons to be learned from Taylor in a recent training session with financial advisors and was asked the question: "What personal price did Taylor pay to achieve his level of success?" To the surprise of the group, I was able to say "none." Taylor has been married to his wife Shearon for more than 35 years. Together they raised two sons, who have also done very well, and he is very close to them. Taylor was able to be true to his values throughout his career.

A large part of Taylor's success was his well-deserved reputation for integrity. He never compromised his integrity for business; people intuitively trusted him and he lived up to their expectations to deserve their trust. In his 30 years in the business, doing as much business as has been done by any financial advisor, he had a flawless compliance record.

In 2002, Taylor retired from the large, national financial services firm that he started with, after more than 30 years of service. Ted Turner offered him a job as his chief operating officer of Turner Enterprises. Taylor was ready to take his career to a new and different level after reaching the "very top" of his profession. Taylor's legacy to financial services lives on through his team, which is now led by Art and Austin.

15

Henry Camp: Going from Good to Great

HENRY CAMP IS a top advisor, but the way he reached this level is different from any of the other top advisors featured in this book. Henry started out the way most top advisors do, but then he reached a plateau that took him 15 years to move beyond. During this time, he lost both his focus and his early momentum. Ultimately, Henry was able to work through these issues, and when he resumed his journey in his fifteenth year in the business, he eventually attained top advisor status. In a 10-year period, he grew his business from $700,000 to $3.5 million and had billions of dollars of corporate assets under management. His evolution transpired by employing the same success principles that our other top advisors share.

Henry's story should be an inspiration to any advisor, but especially to those who have found their business on a plateau and want to take their business to the next level. Fifteen years into the business, Henry made the decision that he wanted to move from being a good advisor to being a great one. His motivational story proves that it is entirely possible to transcend from average to greatness in this industry.

Meet Henry Camp

Henry grew up in a small town outside of Atlanta, Georgia, and graduated from Auburn University in Alabama. He married while in college and got his first job as a banker in Atlanta in the mid-1970s. Henry had higher ambitions and began to focus his interest toward managing municipal bonds for the bank. The more he learned about the brokerage business, the more it appealed to him as a career. He made a career change, leaving banking and moving to E. F. Hutton in 1977.

Henry did not receive any formal training from his manager or the firm. "They didn't know what I was doing and I had no direction," he says. "But what I did have was fear: the fear of not being able to support my wife, who was due with our first child. That fear motivated me to call a lot of people and ask them for their business. I started prospecting in small towns because I thought they would be friendlier and I might have a chance to talk to them."

Henry got his first break when one of his prospects called him back and placed an order for 20,000 shares of Southern Company. Henry's confidence grew; he was not afraid to call for appointments with bigger and bigger prospects, and he had success because of his willingness to meet them face-to-face. He built the foundation of his practice by selling municipal bonds and utility stocks. In Henry's words, "I built my business going to see people, asking them for their business, and then offering them tax-free bonds. In those days, there were a lot of new issues coming out. I found that I never offended anyone by asking if they wanted to look at a local municipal bond offering."

In his first year, Henry did $100,000 in business, which even by today's standards would be considered a successful first year. However, he began to grow dissatisfied by the lack of direction from his firm and decided to make a change to another large financial services firm. Henry was assigned to a small office in Atlanta, and he essentially had to start over: Many of his larger relationships already had accounts with other advisors at his new firm.

Henry persevered and started to prospect the same way as when he was with Hutton, and once again he was successful. For the next six years Henry grew his business to $300,000, but his business began to plateau. The energy in the office was negative, and the growth spurt tapered off.

Before long, Henry lost his early motivation for growing his business. He would come up with a new business idea and go to lunch with some of the other advisors in his office, and by the end of lunch they had thrown so much cold water on his idea that he would return to his office with his shoulders slumped and not bother trying his idea. He says, "The mental aspect of this business is the most important aspect. Your subconscious is so powerful, [and] it can be powerful on the positive side or powerful on the negative side. And I let it be powerful for me on the negative side."

Henry got a new manager who challenged him directly. He told Henry that he had the talent to be a big producer, but didn't have a strong enough commitment to take his business to the next level. Henry realized that he was too much in his comfort zone to care about being a million-dollar producer. He realized that many of his peers were now more successful than he was. "I thought that I can't live the next 20 years being an underachiever, not reaching the professional goals that I know I was capable of. I had to do something about it, so I went and talked to my manager," Henry recalls. "I told him that I didn't feel good about what I was doing, and I didn't know how to get out of this slump. I felt like I had to be proud of what I was doing and proud of myself."

Henry came to the conclusion that the only way to change his circumstances was to change himself, and that change started with his mindset. He realized that in 15 years he had become an average performer; professionally, he had been in neutral, not growing his business at the rate he was capable of: "I've always believed that there are two kinds of people in the world—feelers and doers. Feelers do things when they emotionally feel like it. Doers decide they have a goal and are passionate about the goal, yet their emotional side does not affect their actions. I needed to become a doer."

More important, Henry wanted professional respect. In his words, "People respected me, but they didn't see me as a top advisor. I saw guys passing me every day, becoming million-dollar producers, and I wasn't one of them."

The Transition

Within several weeks of his self-evaluation, the same manager approached Henry and asked him to head up the financial planning initiative for the office. Henry had found his opportunity to succeed and improve his standing in the office, and he jumped on it. He worked hard to motivate himself and the other advisors to get behind the office's financial planning efforts, and the campaign placed his office as one of the best in the country. The manager was so impressed with Henry's work that he offered him the job to be his producing sales manager. Henry accepted the job and was glowing with the feeling of success; he wanted to apply his newfound motivation to his business, as well as being a sales manager.

One day his office friends came and invited him to lunch, as they did almost every day. This time Henry responded, "You know what, guys, I'm not going to lunch with you. I want to take my business to the next level and become a million-dollar producer, and I can't have lunch with you because I don't have time, and we never talk about anything positive." This was a watershed event for Henry because he finally got it off his chest and made the statement. Henry's friends weren't offended; in fact, they understood his new commitment, even though they weren't ready to make the change that Henry was making.

Once he made this statement, Henry felt he really had to go for it. Over the next two years the office did extremely well under Henry's leadership, but his business was not growing the way he wanted. His new challenge was time: Being a great sales manager meant he had less time to grow his own business. He realized to reach a million dollars in business he would have to focus all his time and energy on growing his practice. He resigned as sales manager and told his manager that he needed to focus all his energy on becoming a successful producer.

The Transformation

Henry realized he had to move out of his comfort zone to take his business to the next level. He had been at it for 20 years and was doing $700,000 in business, certainly good, but not yet great. The first step he took was to start visualizing being a million-dollar producer. He started to picture himself in the corner office earning the respect of his peers and more importantly respecting himself professionally

Next, Henry set new goals for himself, focusing on what he really wanted and believed in. He had to visualize what it takes to get there—he had to visualize himself reaching his goals. Henry started to feel the emotion of being a million-dollar producer. He started repeating his own mantra: *I am a million-dollar producer, there's no way I'm not.* "Once I really believed in my goal, there was no turning back," he says.

Henry did $975,000 within 12 months of resigning as sales manager, growing his business by almost 50 percent. He did it by "blocking and tackling," which is how he refers to good time management and a renewed focus on building his business. He also made three big changes during the next year that made an even bigger difference.

First, Henry requested to change where he sat in the office, and he wanted to be moved next to the most successful advisor. He told his manager, "He and I do business totally different, but I just love the guy's energy level and his enthusiasm, and I want to be next to that." Henry spent the first 15 years of his career sitting next to naysayers; now he wanted to be next to someone that was going to lift him up every day and help drive him to do more business. Henry was developing the "mindset" of a top producer through his new work ethic, building confidence, setting goals, and focusing his energy. A big step in this direction was moving away from negativity and toward the positive influence and energy of the office's most successful financial advisor.

Next, he hired two assistants above what the firm provided. This move cost Henry $100,000 out of his pocket. "People thought I was absolutely crazy," he says, "that I wasn't doing enough business to justify this expense. But I would tell them that I'm not a $975,000 producer; I'm a $2.5 million producer. If I grow my business by $700,000 next year, I'll have more than enough money to pay two assistants, with plenty left over."

Henry's decision to spend such a large amount of money "out of pocket" is a clear example of the success principle lesson of long-term orientation. Henry was looking out two to three years and was willing to spend money in the short term with the "bet" that his investment would pay off in the long term, with a significant increase in business. It was another example of the top advisor mindset demonstrating vision, confidence, and risk taking.

Last, Henry added a young advisor to his growing team. Henry noticed this advisor across from his office working extremely hard and saw that he was very good on the phone; he was a good prospector. According to Henry, "I knew I couldn't be a $2.5 million producer by myself, so I hired this young advisor to be part of my team." Henry told his new partner his job was to get him in front of affluent investors, because Henry knew if he could get in front of them he would do business. His new partner did the initial cold calling, making appointments for Henry with affluent prospects. He also made calls to bring prospects to the periodic seminars that Henry was giving. With this new partner now part of his team, Henry was finally able to do what all our top advisors do, which is spending the majority of their time with their best clients and developing relationships with affluent prospects. The "team" lesson was being implemented as part of Henry's transformation into a top advisor.

Henry started to work his existing book with the centers of influence he had as clients. One of his clients was a top insurance agent. They had an excellent relationship, so Henry said to this client, "You know, I'm really motivated to grow my practice, and the only way I can is by getting new clients. If you run across any affluent people, I would appreciate if you would introduce them to me." Since this client wasn't interested in the investment side of the business, he started to send some really strong prospects Henry's way. At the same time, Henry started to call several CPAs he had done business with in the past and told them that he needed their help. By being proactive and leveraging the goodwill he had already created with these referral sources, he was starting to implement the "professional referral network" lesson.

Henry networked with the clients that he already had, leveraging his good relationship with them so that they would introduce him to people they felt he should know and could help. Henry had done a good job of investing their money in conservative investments that performed well over time. He had built a good reputation and relationship with his clients, and not all of them were rich, but they believed in Henry. When he started to ask for referrals they delivered. "My clients who have stuck with me for 20 years would have been embarrassed not to give me a referral when I finally started asking," he says. Eventually he approached his largest client, a multimillion-dollar relationship he acquired in his early years, about sending him referrals. Henry had done a good job of investing his money and they had developed a good relationship. This client once told Henry's wife, "I'm sure there are people at Henry's firm that may be smarter than Henry, but he has kept me out of trouble over the years and we've had good returns, and that means more to me than anything else." Henry had always followed the lesson of focusing on the relationship; he had just never leveraged those good relationships before. He was, however, sitting on a gold mine of goodwill, and once he started to dig, what he unearthed turned out to be priceless.

Henry discovered some key insights during his transformation that were critical to his continued growth. He began to understand how leverage in this business is related to the size of the relationship, and so he focused more and more on larger relationships. In Henry's words, "I gave away all my small accounts, two or three hundred of them, to a couple of young guys. I followed the theory that I had to give the lower part of my book away to grow to the next level." Like all top advisors, he discovered the "leverage of size" success principle and found that fewer but more affluent relationships actually translate to more business. Just as importantly, he discovered that focusing on fewer relationships gave him more time to be proactive in his marketing efforts.

He also realized the importance of time management. Henry had never paid attention to how he spent his time, but now he was obsessed with it. "I realized what I did with the 24 hours in each day was the most critical part of my success," he says. "How I managed those 24 hours would determine if I was going to be a million or a two million-dollar producer. So I started a new policy: I never went out to lunch unless it was with a client or prospect. If I didn't have a client or prospect appointment, I ate at my desk and would be on the phone while I was eating. Once I got into the office I never wanted to lose my momentum or my focus. I trained my colleagues, my friends, and clients not to waste my time, and I did it in an inoffensive way. I became an expert at not letting people steal my time. Can you imagine walking into an attorney's office and just sitting down and saying 'let's shoot the breeze for an hour'? He'd reach over and punch the clock; [attorneys] wouldn't let you steal their time." Like all top advisors, Henry was becoming a master of the time management success principle, making each minute of every day count. He found that over the course of the year, keeping a tight and organized schedule had a significant impact on his success.

Henry realized through this process that he had to make radical changes to make radical improvements in his business, saying, "You don't make small changes and double your business; you make big changes and you double your business." In the third year of his transformation, Henry did $2.5 million, tripling his business in three years. He had met and exceeded all of his goals, yet Henry had just started his transformation.

Becoming a Specialist

The catalyst for beginning the next stage of his career was Henry's ability to turn a bad situation into a good one. Henry was able to get a high-potential mortgage company that had problems with his firm in the past to join his client list. He actually inherited this relationship after the advisor that had opened this account had been terminated from the firm. Henry targeted the top-10 employees of this mortgage company and started developing relationships with them. Aside from securing these individual accounts, Henry set his goal to do more business with the company. There were challenges with this relationship because of the past problems. But he stuck with them, nurtured the business, and ended up securing the larger business account. Eventually, this firm developed into a very significant relationship.

Through this experience, Henry developed expertise in working with corporate executives and providing corporate services. Like so many of our top advisors, Henry had backed into the specialization lesson. He didn't start out knowing anything about corporate services, but through the process of cultivating, nurturing, and developing this problem relationship into a significant account, he became an expert in corporate services.

At the same time, another successful team in his office had also begun developing corporate relationships with companies in Atlanta. This second team was instrumental in helping a large private company go public, and they ended up getting the 401(k) and stock option plan from the company. This same team had also been introduced to another private company going public. This time they didn't succeed in getting the underwriting, but in the process they were selected to handle the stock option plan after the company did go public.

The second team knew Henry from his sales manager days and respected him for the transformation he made in his own business. They also knew that he had developed a level of expertise in corporate services. So they approached Henry and his partner to join their team. Henry agreed that together they could form the best corporate services team in the country—which they eventually did.

The deal was consummated, the business splits determined, and the responsibilities assigned. Henry and one of the senior partners from the other team focused on the corporate services side of the business while the two remaining partners focused on the executives and other affluent clients in the practice. Henry and his new partner identified high-potential private companies and existing public companies and started to pitch the equity compensation and stock option business. They soon became national leaders. Better still, their business exploded.

The team relied heavily on research, focusing on large companies. Henry and his partner started to attend industry trade meetings, and they realized that every year there would be a couple of big conferences on stock option plans. They would attend, stand in their booth, and talk to people from all these companies. Inevitably, the HR director from a large public company would stop by and say, "You know, some time in the next year or so we're probably going to look at different options for our plans; right now ABC financial is running our plan." And Henry would say, "We represent XYZ financial and would love an opportunity to show you what our firm has to offer." Henry found that it wasn't that hard to get the appointment because that was why people were there attending these industry shows—to look for potential providers. Once they got the appointment and discovered the potential client's needs and shared their expertise, Henry and his partner kept dripping on them just like an individual prospect, and in most cases, because of their expertise and specialization, over time they got the business.

Henry and his partner identified senior executives and would cold call them using the following script:

> "Mr./Ms. Senior Executive, my name is Henry Camp and I co-manage a team in Atlanta which is a niche group within our firm XYZ Financial called corporate and institutional advisory services, our focus is on the equity compensation business and we are one of the most experienced teams in our firm in serving the corporate services market. I would appreciate the opportunity to introduce myself to you personally so that if you are ever in the market for another provider you would know about us and our expertise and offerings."

Because of their expertise and specialization they were successful at getting appointments and eventually doing business with many of the top companies in the country.

Henry's team stood out because they were relentless in working to make their team the best corporate services group in the country.

They held a meeting every week for three years to develop their corporate services model. They had a mission statement and a team flowchart structure of the team; they had every process institutionalized into their practice. They also learned to leverage the experts in their firm, especially during presentations to corporations. Henry and his team knew corporate services well enough to make the introductions and pitch their services, but when these presentations got technical and there would be hundreds of questions, they needed to rely on the firm's experts for many of the technical questions.

The Bottom Line

Henry always had the potential to be a top advisor, but like people do, he became distracted by the obstacles in the business. He lost his motivation because he had reached a financial comfort level and allowed himself to be influenced by the many negative forces that can exist in this business. Whereas in the early years he was proactive, soon he was just reacting to the needs of his clients. Consequently, Henry took a 15-year hiatus from being on the top advisor track, but eventually his top advisor mindset emerged and his pride and self-confidence overwhelmed his complacency. Henry eventually did $3.5 million in production and was recognized as one of the top advisors in his firm.

If you have become frustrated knowing that your business is not living up to your potential and believe that you are capable of doing far more business, then Henry's story contains many lessons on how to reignite and develop your latent "top advisor" potential. Even if you have never experienced the career plateau that Henry has, or are just starting out in the business, his story illustrates how the lessons of top advisors can work when applied to developing a better, more lucrative financial services practice.

16

The Asset Challenge

THE PURPOSE OF this book is to enable you to learn from our top advisors and to implement their best practices, taking your business to a significantly higher level. You should now be familiar with the strategies that define the 13 lessons, and understand how our top advisors implemented them into their own businesses. Their personal examples specifically highlighted many of the tactics that worked for them.

The word tactics comes from a military term used to describe "the steps that need to be taken to execute the strategic plan." Too often, training in our industry is focused on just the strategy. This chapter will supply you with the information on the necessary tactics that can bring the 13 strategies to life.

The idea behind the Asset Challenge was developed by a regional manager I worked with back in 2006. He believed that by setting a high asset goal and identifying and training highly motivated advisors, a goal of $50 million worth of business could be achieved. I was recruited to be part of the training team and was assigned the task of putting together a tactical process.

Over the course of that year, I saw many advisors reach this goal after following the training we provided. These training techniques were then validated by my interviews with our 15 top advisors, many of whom consistently brought in at least $50 million in net new assets every year. This is why I believe that any advisor who can master the success principles and these specific strategies can bring in significant net new assets within 12 months of reading this book. All you have to provide is the motivation to implement the tactical strategies outlined in this chapter.

One caveat for the Asset Challenge is that your goal should be based on the size of the investable assets of your average client. The amount of assets brought in each year will depend on the experience level of the advisors and the minimum size of the relationships they work with. None of our top advisors started with minimum relationships of $1 million or more

These tactical strategies should help you bring in at least 12 new affluent relationships a year. For example, if your minimum asset size is currently $250,000, and the average new relationship brought in is $500,000, and twelve new relationships were acquired over a 12-month period, then this would result in $6 million in new client assets. By following the tactics for bringing in new assets from existing clients (which will be described later in the chapter), you should be able to bring in an additional $6 million, totaling $12 million of new assets.

However, if an advisor has a minimum of $500,000 for new client relationships and the average account size is $1 million, and the advisor acquires 12 new relationships, then the total assets for new relationships would be $12 million. That amount, combined with tactics for bringing in new assets of $12 million from existing clients, means they could reach a $25 million Asset Challenge. For those who have a minimum size of $1 million for new client relationships and the average account size is $2.5 million and they acquire 12 new relationships, then the total assets for new relationships would be $30 million. Combine that amount with tactics for bringing in $20 million from existing clients, and they could reach $50 million in new assets.

Tactical Strategy #1: Client Referrals

Referrals are the second most effective strategy for bringing in millionaire clients, and the number-one strategy that financial advisors use to acquire new relationships. While most advisors rely on unsolicited referrals from their clients, they are usually surprised and generally frustrated that they don't get as many as they feel they deserve. It is not a matter of a client's unwillingness: As I've said before, client surveys usually indicate that satisfied clients are very willing to provide referrals. The problem is that many clients just don't think about providing referrals, even though they may be willing to do so. Another issue is that clients may believe that their advisor is too busy to accept new clients.

The tactic for best implementing this strategy is developing and implementing a proactive referral plan into your practice. It isn't enough just to ask for a referral; the next step is to make it easy for the clients to provide the introductions. Clients need to be made aware that you are looking for referrals. They also need your help teaching them how identify and introduce you to a referral.

Another aspect of this tactic is to have the right mindset, as discussed throughout this book. Our top advisors all believe in themselves and are confident that they are the best in the business in regards to helping clients achieve their investment goals. The top advisors don't ask, they *offer* to help their friends, family, and work associates. In many ways they feel like financial missionaries, not salespeople. I would urge you to adopt the same mindset as you "offer to help," and not "ask" for referrals.

The cornerstone of making this tactical strategy work is having satisfied clients. If your clients are happy these tactics will work; if they are not, then the strategy will fail. The drivers of client satisfaction and retention will be covered later in this chapter, and these drivers must be implemented into a retention strategy for the client referrals tactic to work.

Make a referral offer part of your "agenda," either by using the examples of proactive referral scripts provided in Chapter 6 on "Marketing Best Practices" or developing your own script. More important than the actual words in the script is that a proactive referral request is made to every client at least once a year, and that the right mindset is employed. When the proactive agenda referral method is used with each client in combination with client events, then you are making it easy for each client to introduce you to other affluent people they know. Once again, I recommend holding at least 12 client events each year; these events should be a combination of fun and investment strategy sessions.

All potential referral sources should be reminded in a professional way about your new relationship minimums. You can use the following line: "Mr./Ms. Prospect, in thinking of people we can help most, we have found we are most effective with individuals who have investable assets of at least _____."

LESSONS USED IN TACTICAL STRATEGY #1

- *Mindset:* Be confident in yourself and your ability to make a positive difference with affluent clients.

- *Long-Term Orientation:* Set a goal to incorporate a proactive referral process with each client once a year.

❑ *Marketing:* Apply the client referral and client event tactics.

❑ *Commitment to Service:* Most clients will become "raving fans" if a real commitment to proactive client service is made.

❑ *Wealth Management:* Most affluent clients prefer the wealth-management process and will be most likely to refer people to advisors that use that approach.

❑ *Time Management:* Devote specific time blocks each day to implement a proactive referral process and client events.

RESULTS FOR TACTICAL STRATEGY #1

This strategy should generate at least 12 qualified referrals a year, of which at least four should turn into clients. The total assets from these new clients should be in the range of $1 million to $10 million, depending on the minimum size of new relationships.

Tactical Strategy #2:
Professional Referral Network

Millionaires find financial advisors often through their CPA and/or their attorney. Because of the importance of finance-related decisions and the uncertainty of the outcome, wealthy investors will be very careful about establishing a new investment relationship, so they will rely on the trust and credibility of their existing CPA and/or attorney relationship. As I mentioned in Chapter 7 on "Professional Referral Networks," it takes 10 influencer appointments to get one referral source.

The average top advisor has at least three different influencer sources of referrals. This should be your goal. To achieve this, you will need to meet, face-to-face, with 30 different influencers, using the follow-up process described in Chapter 7. Both the appointment and follow-up process are required for this strategy to work. To find these influencers, start with your own clients' CPAs and attorneys. This tactical strategy requires patience and a lot of upfront work to develop the confidence of the referral source, but the payoff is well worth the time.

LESSONS USED IN TACTICAL STRATEGY #2

☐ *Specialization:* Sharing your specialization and expertise with a potential referral source will make you an attractive referral.

☐ *Wealth Management:* The wealth-management process will have a high level of appeal to professional referral sources and will lead to actual referrals.

☐ *Long-Term Orientation:* Setting a goal for meeting with 30 potential referral sources is required to create a network of three professionals who will consistently provide referrals. This process takes patience and a long-term orientation, because it might take 12 months to 18 months before you get the first referral.

☐ *Time Management:* A real commitment to time invested in this process is required for it to work. Scheduling time every week to implement this strategy is a necessity.

RESULTS FOR TACTICAL STRATEGY #2

The conversion rate for turning a referral from an influencer into a client is at least 80 percent. It is high because influencers usually give referrals in "money-in-motion" situations or when their clients have need for an advisor. If each of your three influencers provides two qualified referrals a year, then the result should be the addition of at least four new affluent clients annually. Depending on your minimum new relationship size, you should generate between $1 million and $10 million in total new assets.

Tactical Strategy #3: Client Events

Client events offer a perfect way of allowing your clients to help you. Most "raving fan" clients are willing to provide referrals to their financial advisor, but one of the biggest challenges for them is coming up with names of people to refer. Hosting fun events around your clients' outside interests is a great way to meet their friends. Most people associate with other people who enjoy the same outside activities, are the same age, and have similar economic status. Inviting clients to an event they would enjoy and encouraging them to bring along a friend with a similar interest is a nonthreatening way to get your clients to make an introduction.

The second part of the client event equation is having regularly scheduled investment strategy sessions. In these sessions you should give an overview of the current market environment and how investors can be best positioned and then also provide an overview of your wealth-management process. The reason these sessions are so important is that they provide an easy transition between the personal and business relationship. The investment strategy session becomes a "catchall" in which personal friends, prospects, and new referrals can be introduced to your wealth-management approach in a nonthreatening way. Chapter 6 covers in detail the tactics that should be employed in the effective use of client events as a marketing strategy.

LESSONS USED IN TACTICAL STRATEGY #3

- *Mindset:* Setting up client events requires strategic planning, energy, and a solid work ethic.

- *Commitment to Service:* Clients must be "loyal" and "happy" to want to help their advisor, and for that to happen, the advisor must be committed to providing outstanding, proactive customer service.

- *Relationship Focus:* Developing relationships with prospects at client events is not only the goal, but a requirement for the successful implementation of this strategy

- *Wealth Management:* The wealth-management process should be showcased at investment strategy sessions.

RESULTS FOR TACTICAL STRATEGY #3

This tactical strategy should be used in combination with the client referral strategy and, if implemented, should increase the number of affluent clients acquired by 50 percent, increasing the number from four to six. Depending on the minimum size of your relationships, this tactical strategy should result in incremental assets of between $1 million and $5 million.

Tactical Strategy #4: Niche Marketing

Niche marketing is the most effective way to market in financial services. It is based on the concept that financial advisors are "insiders" or part of the niche group they are marketing to. This marketing method requires an immersion into the targeted niche market and the development of a specialization.

Once you identify your target niche market and acquire the expertise, there are two primary ways to leverage your specialization. One is through "warm calling" and the other is networking. Warm calling involves calling affluent individuals within your niche market and making a connection with them by sharing your expertise and experience and providing references. The networking tactic is about putting yourself in the right place to meet affluent individuals in your targeted niche. It's about attending, speaking at, and participating in trade shows, conferences, and association meetings within your niche market. It means identifying who the centers of influence and leaders in a local niche market are, and then building relationships with those individuals. Specific niche market tactics are detailed in Chapter 6.

LESSONS USED IN TACTICAL STRATEGY #4

- *Specialization:* Developing a specialization is a requirement to be an effective niche marketer.

- *Long-Term Orientation:* Create and implement a clear vision for the particular niche you want to build your business around.

- *Professional Development:* The higher the level of expertise obtained, the harder it is for others to compete within your niche.

- *Time Management:* This tactical strategy requires blocking out time for marketing and for ongoing professional growth in order to develop your expertise.

RESULTS FOR TACTICAL STRATEGY #4

Implementation of this tactical strategy should result in at least four new clients within 12 months. Depending on the niche market and the minimum size requirements, the strategy should result in new annual assets of $1 million to $10 million.

Tactical Strategy #5: Right Place, Right People

In real estate, location is everything. This same concept applies to a successful marketing strategy for financial advisors. Right place, right people marketing was the number-one marketing strategy used by our top advisors, and it specifically means putting yourself in the position to meet affluent people, developing relationships with those people, and effectively transitioning from a personal relationship to a business relationship. Developing the right verbal transition lines is the key to making this strategy work. These transition lines are provided in chapters 5, 6 and 8. The specific tactics on how to make this strategy work are outlined in Chapter 6: Marketing Best Practices.

LESSONS USED IN TACTICAL STRATEGY #5

- *Mindset:* The first step in implementing this strategy is determining the best places to find and have access to affluent investors. You also need to have the confidence necessary to approach them once you are in the right place.

- *Relationship Focus:* One of the most important implementation steps is to develop relationships with the affluent individuals you meet by being at the right places.

◻ *Long-Term Orientation:* The development of those personal relationships takes time.

◻ *Time Management:* Set aside time to become intricately involved in the many opportunities that your lifestyle and interests provide.

RESULTS FOR TACTICAL STRATEGY #5

Within 12 months of this strategy's implementation, the transition between the personal and business relationship should start and result in at least four new affluent relationships a year. This should translate into $1 million to $10 million in new assets, depending on your minimum size and the level of access you are able to get to affluent investors.

Tactical Strategy #6: Nonprofit and Outside Interest Leadership

This strategy was covered in detail in Chapter 8. Developing relationships with affluent individuals who are involved with nonprofit organizations and then transitioning, over time, from a personal to a business relationship with them is the foundation on which this tactical strategy is built. However, it could take a year or more before your first affluent client is acquired.

LESSONS USED IN TACTICAL STRATEGY #6

◻ *Mindset:* Being a hard worker and effective communicator, and having high energy and a strong work ethic are all required for this strategy.

◻ *Leverage of Size:* The most affluent individuals in a community are usually involved in nonprofit organizations.

◻ *Long-Term Orientation:* Finding wealthy investors through nonprofit involvement is an effective marketing technique, but it requires patience.

❏ *Time Management:* Taking a leadership position in at least two nonprofit organizations is recommended. Most of the work for these organizations will occur after business hours.

RESULTS FOR TACTICAL STRATEGY #6

For every nonprofit organization that you participate in, you should expect to acquire at least two new affluent relationships within 12 to18 months. Because of the time commitment required for taking a leadership role in these nonprofit organizations, most of our top advisors limited their leadership involvement to no more than two different organizations. Expect to add between $1 million to $10 million total assets if the tactics described in Chapter 8 are followed. The average size of the new relationship has more to do with the profile and cost of entry of the organization than it does your current minimum size.

Tactical Strategy #7:
More Assets from Existing Clients

Getting more assets from current clients will be the easiest assets that you will ever get. The trust relationship is already built, and if your clients are satisfied, then they will be receptive to a discussion about bringing in held-away assets. Client surveys have consistently shown that most clients have as much money held away from their advisors as they have with them. I have seen millions of dollars in assets brought in over a short period of time because new assets were discovered from existing clients, and because an advisor showed clients why it made sense for them to transfer these assets.

Russ Alan Prince validates my own observations and experiences of client assets held away in his book *Cultivating the Middle-Class Millionaire*. This book is based on surveys of millionaire clients and reveals the following information:

❏ Among loyal millionaire clients, 94 percent are very likely to give their primary advisor more assets in the next 12 months.

- Loyal millionaire clients transferred, on average, $376,000 of new assets in the past 12 months to their primary advisor.

- Slightly more than one-quarter—26 percent—of millionaires have all their assets with one advisor; the higher the net worth, the lower percentage of having only one advisor.

- Only 12 percent of millionaire clients were asked by their advisor for more assets to invest during the past 12 months.

- Among financial advisors, 81.6 percent believe they have all their millionaire client assets.

The problem is that most advisors don't know how to ask, and they don't have a proactive process in their practice to discover and acquire their clients' assets held away. Tactical Strategy #7, when implemented, will solve both problems.

The first step is the discovery of what assets are held away. This conversation should not be a separate meeting, but part of an annual planning/review session in which you position the importance of knowing about assets held away. Every year you should begin this conversation so that you can be updated on any new assets that might have come in. This conversation can happen initially during a quarterly review, if you want to get started on this strategy before the annual review occurs.

You can easily explain that unless you know about all of the client's assets, it is impossible to allocate the assets you are currently investing. The outside assets must be taken into account for the correct allocation that matches with the client's risk tolerance. The client should be reminded that 90 percent of the portfolio's success can be related to the proper asset allocation. Here is an example of how you might raise this issue:

"Mr./Ms. S, if I am doing my job correctly, my relationship with you should go beyond just advising you on the assets you have at our firm. As you know, asset allocation is a core part of our wealth-management process, and I am comfortable that the assets you hold with me are properly allocated. However, I need to have an idea of how the assets you have with me relate to the asset allocation that you have at other places. It gives me the perspective and context that enables me to do the best possible job I can for you. I would also like to encourage you, as you feel comfortable, to consider consolidating all of your assets with me, so I can include everything in our wealth-management process and simplify your financial life. Let's take a minute and allow me to build out your balance sheet."

Once the assets held away are disclosed, then you can determine exactly what the total opportunity is for additional assets from existing clients. A strategy should be developed for each client for bringing the away assets in.

The strategy, along with the assets held away, should be put in the client file to be referenced throughout the year. You can keep a spreadsheet of assets held away, charting the progress made throughout the year. This is a perfect example of the power of a proactive daily process that, over time, will make a significant difference in your practice. The monthly contact or quarterly reviews are the opportunity to execute the strategy and make the case on why assets held away should be managed by the advisor.

Examples of why clients should consolidate all their assets could include:

◻ Better reporting

◻ Total asset allocation

◻ Simplicity for the client

◻ Lower fees

▢ Opportunity for additional products and services

If you treat your clients' assets "held away" as if they were with you and advise them accordingly, you will be successful in bringing those assets into your practice.

LESSONS USED IN TACTICAL STRATEGY #7

▢ *Mindset:* Goal orientation is important when using this strategy: Between 30 percent and 50 percent of the new assets should come from keeping your eye on this prize.

▢ *Relationship Focus:* For this strategy to work clients must be loyal and willing to disclose and eventually transfer assets held away.

▢ *Wealth Management:* Asset allocation is a fundamental part of the wealth-management process and provides the rationale for building a total balance sheet of a client's assets—including assets held away.

▢ *Time Management:* The discovery, implementation, and tracking components of this strategy all take time, but it is probably the most efficient use of time that an advisor can make.

▢ *Commitment to Service:* If clients feel they are taken care of, they will be willing to transfer in assets held away.

RESULTS FOR TACTICAL STRATEGY #7

The results of this strategy will be based primarily on the number of affluent clients and total assets currently under management. The goal should be to bring in at least 20 percent of the total assets held away each year. If properly implemented, this tactical strategy should account for 30 percent to 50 percent of new assets brought in. The range, depending on your current total assets and number of clients, should be between $6 million and $20 million or more a year of additional assets.

Tactical Strategy #8:
Product and Service Expansion

Offering multiple products and services is part of the wealth-management process that our top advisors use. Details of this strategy were provided in Chapter 11, but the main technique involves developing a list of potential product and service expansion opportunities. Affluent clients want "one-stop shopping" and appreciate a financial advisor who offers a wide range of products and services that are appropriate to their needs. Expanding the financial products and services that each affluent client has is a win-win situation for both the client and the advisor. This philosophy accomplishes three important things:

- It simplifies the client's life by having all of the person's financial needs handled by one advisor.

- It increases the advisor's business.

- It keeps the client tied to the advisor.

My experience has shown that if clients have five or more different products and services, they will do three times more business than clients with only two or three products. There is also evidence that clients with six or more different products and services have a near-perfect retention rate (99 percent).

Tactically, this strategy can be implemented as follows:

- Determine which financial products and services your clients should be exposed to.

- Commit to learning about those selected products and services.

- Expose clients to the selected products and services through your monthly contact system.

- Set up an internal tracking system to ensure that each client is exposed to at least six different appropriate products and services.

- Develop a minimum amount of business that each client should do each year. Develop a strategy for those clients doing less than the minimum by exposing them to a broad range of different products and services.

LESSONS USED IN TACTICAL STRATEGY #8

- *Mindset:* Set a goal for expanding the number of products and services each client has to six new products. This target will directly affect how you increase your business and how you make decisions on retaining existing clients.

- *Professional Growth:* Willingness to expose clients to different noninvestment products and services (e.g., insurance, college savings funds, banking-related services) requires the financial advisor to acquire knowledge about these different types of accounts.

- *Service Commitment:* Loyal clients will be willing to do more business and consolidate all their financial needs with one advisor.

- *Wealth Management:* Integrating all of the client's financial needs into a comprehensive plan is the core of the wealth-management process.

RESULTS FOR TACTICAL STRATEGY #8

If you commit to providing your clients with a full range of different financial products and services, it can result in a total business increase of 5–10 basis points (bps) of total assets under management. The amount of basis points will be dependent on the total number of assets you have. The higher the total number of assets, the lower the basis point increase. However, a 10 basis point increase on $100 million total asset base could generate an additional $100,000 in business. The higher the affluence of each individual client, the more significant the business increase could be. The goal is for each client to have six different appropriate financial products and services.

Tactical Strategy #9:
The Monthly Client Contact

The process of calling every significant client relationship on a proactive basis, at least once a month, ties in all the different tactical strategies. The purpose of the monthly contact is to increase client satisfaction and give the advisor the opportunity to execute the other tactical strategies.

Every year, each of your clients should receive eight monthly contacts, three quarterly contacts, and one annual review. This schedule can best be accomplished if you can manage your business within a range of 100 total client relationships. There are four objectives for each contact:

1. Reconnect with the client from the last contact—typically on a personal level.

2. Review the client's investment portfolio in the context of the current market and long-term plan.

3. Execute a tactical strategy for marketing leverage (i.e., the client referral process, your influencer network, client event invitation, new asset strategy, or expansion).

4. Ask if there is "anything else" on the client's mind.

The proactive monthly contact is the primary factor related to the client-retention strategy that is outlined in more detail in Chapter 12. The following sample script shows how you can engage your clients without sounding redundant month after month. (As you read the script, you'll see how different parts of the script accomplish the four objectives.)

Proactive Monthly Contact Script

"Hello Mr./Ms. Client, this is Joe Johnson. I wanted to check in with you to give you an update on your investment portfolio.

Is this a convenient time? Good.

"Before the portfolio update, I remember you telling me that your family had scheduled a vacation in Hawaii last month. How did that go? *(Reconnection)*

"Your portfolio looks fine, and since our last conversation I don't have any additional recommendations to make. As I mentioned during our last conversation, we expect a great deal of volatility in the short term, but I feel we are well positioned to take advantage of the market as I believe it will start to recover later in the year. Do you have any questions or concerns as it relates to your investment portfolio? *(Investment Review)*

"I also wanted to invite you to a golf outing [or any other outside interest activity] later this month on [give specifics of time and place]. During our annual review, I had mentioned that I wanted to invite you to some fun events as a way to spend more time with you, but also to have the opportunity to meet individuals that you think I should meet as prospective clients, who would also enjoy golf. This would only be an opportunity for me to meet your guest and see if there is a potential connection. Does anyone come to mind that you could invite to join us? *(Marketing Leverage)*

"Is there anything else on your mind that we haven't discussed that I could help you with, or suggestions on how we could improve any aspect of our business with you? *('Anything Else' Question)*"

The annual review is a significantly expanded version of the monthly contact, and this meeting should incorporate the following topics:

◻ Long-term goals, objectives, and risk-tolerance review

- Portfolio and asset allocation review and recommendations

- Liability management discussion

- Asset protection review

- Estate planning

- Balance sheet, asset allocation

- Service feedback

- CPA and estate attorney partnership

- Referrals—offer to help

- Questions and other issues

- Next steps

LESSONS USED IN TACTICAL STRATEGY #9

- *Mindset:* Having a goal-oriented mindset is required to maintain a consistent proactive monthly contact with the top affluent clients.

- *Commitment to Service:* The monthly contact and the quarterly and annual reviews are primary tactics for leveraging the existing client relationship for business growth.

- *Relationship Focus:* Affluent clients want to know you care about them beyond their investments. Bonding on a personal level can best be achieved at the beginning or the end of a conversation. This personal bonding is important to your clients and should be part of the monthly contact structure.

- *Wealth Management:* The monthly contact is an ideal time to introduce and expose clients to different products and services that are appropriate to expand the relationships.

❑ *Time Management:* With the ideal number of 100 affluent clients, you will need to make a commitment to contacting five to six different clients a day. If you average in the extra time needed for quarterly and annual reviews, then there is a time commitment of two to three hours each day.

RESULTS FOR TACTICAL STRATEGY #9

This tactical strategy ties all the other strategies together and is the catalyst that drives the results of all the strategies. By itself, making monthly client contact doesn't add assets or business, but without this strategy the results of the others wouldn't happen. Regular contact also contributes to the relationship development of your clients and moving them all toward the coveted "raving fan" status.

Tactical Strategy #10: Client Retention

Highly affluent clients are too hard to get for you not to have a retention strategy. I have seen so many advisors who did a good job of acquiring new affluent clients, but didn't have existing satisfied and loyal clients, so they ended up losing as many clients as they brought in. Chapter 12 reviews the importance of a commitment to service and provides the details of developing and maintaining a good client-retention strategy. The important point for the Asset Challenge is that these are net assets, not new assets. Net assets means assets lost subtracted from new assets gained. Acquiring $25 million in new assets and forfeiting $15 million in existing client relationships can turn a $25 million Asset Challenge into a $10 million one.

The four drivers of retention are:

❑ Proactive client contact (monthly)

❑ Expansion of products and services

❑ Good performance relative to goals

❑ Resolution of problems

LESSONS USED IN TACTICAL STRATEGY #10

◻ *Mindset:* Many advisors have asset and business goals, but top advisors also have retention goals.

◻ *Relationship Focus:* Time must be spent with your clients to keep them satisfied and develop them into loyal clients.

◻ *Service Commitment:* Proactive service takes ordinary service and turns it into extraordinary service, and that's what it takes to keep affluent clients.

◻ *Wealth Management:* Affluent clients with six or more different products and services with you will have an extremely high retention rate.

◻ *Team:* The client associate plays a pivotal role in providing outstanding service to your affluent clients.

◻ *Long-Term Orientation:* Client service doesn't result in short-term business, but it is essential for long-term growth.

◻ *Time Management:* Time must be invested in the client relationship for your clients to be satisfied and ultimately loyal.

RESULTS FOR TACTICAL STRATEGY #10

The goal of this strategy is to not lose existing clients or assets, or at the least lose the fewest number possible. The only numbers that count are the net numbers (gain minus loses). Some client attrition is inevitable, but the goal is to lose less than 5 percent per year.

Tactical Strategy #11:
Prospect Pipeline Management

The tactical strategies for acquiring new affluent clients and assets will get any advisor in front of prospective clients. However, without effective management of prospects in the pipeline, those prospects will not transform into new clients.

The ideal situation is when an advisor meets with prospects and they agree to do business right away. For our top advisors, this happens frequently because of the quality of referrals from clients and their influencer network. However, even the top advisors don't close all of their prospects after the first appointment. The first appointment should be about a discovery process, not a presentation. The second appointment would be about presenting a recommended course of action, based on the discovery of information provided in the first appointment. If, during the first two appointments, the prospect doesn't take the steps to become a client, then the client's name goes into the prospect pipeline.

Once the advisor has entered a qualified prospect (after at least one appointment) in the prospect pipeline, the advisor should be committed to contacting the prospect at least once a month. These monthly contacts should be similar to the monthly contacts with a client, because you will be treating these prospects like they are already your clients. The four components of these contacts are:

1. *Reconnection (Personal or Investment-Related):* The reconnection component could be the result of some relevant information sent to the prospect in advance.

2. *Market Review and Investment Strategy Discussion:* The market review is an update on the advisor's view on the current investment strategy, tailored to the prospect's holdings.

3. *Recommendations Made and Next Steps:* Recommendation is what the advisor suggests the prospect do next. Examples could range from advising the prospect to make a specific investment to extending an invitation to an investment seminar or a social event, or an invitation to create a financial plan.

4. Summary ("Anything Else" Conversation): The summary is to review the next steps and ask the prospect if there is anything else on his mind that either you or his current advisor has not addressed.

If your prospects believe that you are committed to them, will provide a superior wealth-management process, and service them better than their existing advisor, they will move their business your way. Your goal is to position yourself as a strong number-two choice with all the prospects in your pipeline. There is no competition for the number-two position, and over time the prospect's current advisor often will make a mistake, opening the door for the advisor who has a strong pipeline management process in place.

LESSONS USED IN TACTICAL STRATEGY #11

◻ *Mindset:* Confidence, risk taking, and goal setting are all part of generating the motivation to stay in touch with prospects. Because there is potential rejection in the follow-up process, a high level of motivation is required.

◻ *Marketing:* The acquisition of new affluent clients won't happen without a strong prospect pipeline follow-up process.

◻ *Leverage of Size:* The best way to grow your business is to continue to upgrade your prospect pipeline as it relates to the size of the prospects in it.

◻ *Relationship Focus:* Relationship building is the cornerstone of a good prospect follow-up system. If a good relationship is built, in almost all cases the business will follow.

◻ *Long-Term Orientation:* The reason that there is no competition for the number-two spot is that most advisors are not willing to commit the required time to develop a good

relationship with prospects. In most cases, the more affluent the client is, the more time needs to be invested in the
development of the relationship.

☐ *Time Management:* Prospect pipeline management requires
a commitment of time. If there are 50 prospects in the
pipeline, then contacting two to three per day is required—
which translates into about an hour of time daily. This contact should be one of the highest priorities.

RESULTS FOR TACTICAL STRATEGY #11
This is a supporting strategy for the other acquisition tactical
strategies. Without an effective pipeline management process, the
other acquisition strategies will not result in as many new clients
and assets. A good prospect follow-up process will make the difference in whether you reach your Asset Challenge goal.

Tactical Strategy #12: Time Management
As you have seen from the previous lists, time management is integral in each of the tactical strategies. Incorporating the tactical
strategies into your daily practices should not require more time,
but it does necessitate the reallocation of time. The recommendation for experienced advisors is that at least 50 percent of their
time be spent executing the tactical strategies. This time should be
divided almost evenly between client and marketing strategies.

Keep in mind that there is no such thing as a perfect day, and
any ideal schedule will be interrupted. The key is to try to stick
with your schedule 80 percent of the time. The most important
concept here is that the morning is reserved for proactive activities, while the afternoon is more for reactive activities. For new
advisors with fewer clients, the client contact time should be
replaced with marketing contacts and appointments. Even for the
most experienced advisor, building relationships with existing
clients and affluent prospects is the most important activity that

can be done and everything else can be delegated, especially after the wealth-management and investment process is established.

The cornerstones of time management are delegation, prioritization, and time blocking. If these time-management techniques are all used, as described in Chapter 13, then as a financial advisor you will find more time in your day to execute these tactical strategies.

LESSONS USED IN TACTICAL STRATEGY #12

- *Mindset:* Achieving the goals set will be dependent on how time is spent.

- *Marketing:* Time must be spent every day on marketing to build a long-term successful practice.

- *Relationship Focus:* Fifty percent of every day should be spent with clients and prospects.

- *Service Commitment:* Regular proactive contact with clients is a requirement for creating satisfied and loyal clients.

- *Team:* Having a strong team to support you will allow you to spend the majority of your time with clients and prospects.

RESULTS FOR TACTICAL STRATEGY #12

This is a supporting strategy that ties into all the others. The results from the other strategies would be significantly less without good time management. How you spend your time is the biggest determinate of a successful financial services practice.

The Scorecard

When all the tactical strategies and top advisor lessons are brought together and implemented, the annual Asset Challenge can be achieved.

ACQUISITION OF NEW AFFLUENT CLIENTS AND ASSETS

Strategy	Assets Acquired	New Client Acquisition
TACTICAL STRATEGY #1		
Client Referrals	$1–10 million	4 clients
TACTICAL STRATEGY #2		
Professional Referral Network	$1–10 million	4 clients
TACTICAL STRATEGY #3		
Client Events	$1–5 million	2 clients
TACTICAL STRATEGY #4		
Niche Marketing	$1–10 million	4 clients
TACTICAL STRATEGY #5		
Right Place, Right People	$1–3 million	2–4 clients
TACTICAL STRATEGY #6		
Nonprofit Leadership	$1–5 million	2–4 clients
TACTICAL STRATEGY #7		
More Existing Client Assets	$6–20 million	n/a
TOTAL	**$12–63 million**	**18–22 clients**
Provision for Loss (5 percent or less)	**($1–10 million)**	**(5 clients)**
NET TOTAL	**$11–53 million**	**13–17 clients**

Whether your own asset challenge is $10 million or $50 million, the tactical strategies should be viewed as the tools that, if used, will result in achieving an increase in your assets. The number of new clients and assets from each of the strategies could be much higher. I used affluent client acquisition and asset numbers that I was confident could be reached and have seen top advisors far exceed, using a combination of the top advisor lessons and tactical strategies I have shared in this book. Setting an Asset Challenge each year will be an important step to take your business to the next level, but the implementation of the tactical strategies will be the determinate of your success or failure in reaching your goals.

◻ ◻ ◻

I hope that this book has inspired you. As our top advisors can attest, highly motivated individuals can build extraordinary business practices in the financial services industry. I hope, too, that you come away with more than just inspiration, and that you have a clearer vision and roadmap to follow to take your business to the next level and one day become a top advisor yourself.

Printed in the USA
CPSIA information can be obtained
at www.ICGtesting.com
JSHW030335060823
45940JS00004B/15

9 781400 336562